FLY DRESSING

FLY-DRESSING

DAVID J. COLLYER

Foreword by Richard Walker

*With 91 drawings by Derek Bradbury
8 pages of colour plates*

DAVID & CHARLES

NEWTON ABBOT   LONDON
NORTH POMFRET (VT)

To Marjorie, for all she has had to put up
with from me over the years.

British Library Cataloguing in Publication Data

Collyer, David J.
  Fly-dressing.
  1. Fly tying
  I. Title
  688.7'912   SH451

ISBN 0-7153-6719-6

First published 1975
Second impression 1978
Third impression 1980
Fourth impression 1984
Fifth impression 1985

Printed in Great Britain by
Redwood Burn Limited Trowbridge, Wilts
for David & Charles (Publishers) Limited
Brunel House   Newton Abbot   Devon

Published in the United States of America
by David & Charles Inc   North Pomfret   Vermont 05053 USA

CONTENTS

6

7

8

LIST OF COLOUR PLATES

Coachman; Alexandra; Papoose; Cardinal; Harlot; Olive and Gold; Alder; Teal-winged Butcher; Brown Spider; Black and Peacock Spider

Colour photographs by Alistair Dumbell.

ACKNOWLEDGEMENTS

My thanks are due to my good friend Brian Harris of *Angling* magazine for his permission to use extracts from many of my articles which have provided the basis of this book. To Gerry Hughes of *Angler's Mail* for his help and encouragement and to Richard Walker for his flattering comments in his foreword and his always unstinting assistance, not merely to myself but to any angler who approaches him. I should like to thank Derek Bradbury for his beautiful line drawings, without which the book would lose much of its character and finally to that unknown angler at Chew Valley Lake who pushed me into completing the work.

FOREWORD

David Collyer is not only one of the best professional fly-tiers in
the business, he is also an exceptionally capable angler and a good
naturalist. He knows what insects and other water creatures are
eaten by trout; he knows how to imitate them with the materials
available to the fly-tier; and by reason of his trade, the patterns he
devises have to be such as can be tied without great difficulty.

David's considerable ability in casting, including long-distance
work, has necessitated the production of artificial flies that are not
only attractive to the fish, but which are soundly constructed so as
to stand up to severe casting stresses without disintegrating. His
writings for *Angling* magazine bring him letters from readers all
over the world, and with his sure eye for useful new patterns, he
has been able to exploit the best of the suggestions that have come
his way; and his correspondents continue to write because he has
always been meticulous in giving credit to others where it is due.

All this, combined with his exceptional ability to instruct, make
this, his first book, one that will take its place for all time in the
history of fly-tying development.

RICHARD WALKER

INTRODUCTION

During the summer of 1972 I met an angler at Chew Valley lake in Somerset who asked where it was possible to obtain a copy of 'your book', he had apparently tried all his local bookshops with no success. This was not really surprising because the book had not as yet been written!

He said that he read my column in *Angling* magazine each month and naturally assumed that I had had a book published about the various flies I had been writing about there. I then had to admit to him that I was the greatest 'starter' of books in this country – the only trouble I had was in finishing them! At home I had at least four first chapters of books that have never really got off the ground; I must admit that I felt a little guilty because this was not by any means the first time this sort of encounter had occurred. I resolved really to get down to it and this time to go beyond the first chapter and actually finish the book. The following pages are the result; I hope they will provide you, the reader, with entertainment as well as some instruction in the rather peculiar methods of fly-dressing that I employ.

This book is based on the column published in *Angling,* and nearly all the patterns that I have written about there appear in these pages plus some anecdotes and experiences for which there simply was not room in the magazine. The basic reason I had for writing the column – aside from the money! – was to present to the reader a selection of tried, tested and proven fly patterns. It was not intended in any way to be a comprehensive list of flies and their dressings – there are many other books that attempt to do this, and it has been my experience that many of the patterns listed are poor fish-takers if not downright useless. Every single fly in this book has been proven by either my friends or myself to be an effective pattern under the correct circumstances.

There will inevitably be flies which are not listed here which are excellent patterns nonetheless. Perhaps among them will be a favourite of yours; if so I beg your forbearance and I hope that at some time in the future it will be included in a later work. There are certainly other flies that I should have liked to include but either they have had too little time in which to prove themselves or they are adequately covered by other books.

I have tried in this book to run a difficult course – to compile a reference work on flies and their dressings plus any other relevant details concerning their correct use and presentation, and at the same time to tell the story of each pattern and some of my experiences in using them. It should be borne in mind that no fly is the 'ultimate', no pattern will always catch fish and I for one hope that no such fly will ever be designed. The main attraction that fly-fishing holds for me is in its constant testing of my small skill at selecting the fly which is correct for that particular moment and in which the fish will show an interest; mostly I am wrong but as the years pass I slowly learn from my mistakes. In this book and in my column I have tried to provide a short-cut, to eliminate at least some of my errors for the reader's benefit – I hope that I have succeeded.

D.J.C.
Reigate, Surrey   *January 1975*

DRY FLIES

CHAPTER ONE

WINGED DRY FLIES

HACKLEPOINT COACHMAN

This is the pattern of dry fly which has accounted for more fish for me than perhaps any other. I have used it to good effect on many stillwater fisheries in England and Wales but it seems to me that it is at its best on rivers in the late evening. The Coachman in all its forms is generally acknowledged to be a good fish-taking pattern, but when it is tied using white hacklepoint wings I believe this enhances its attraction to the fish. This is because the solid web wings tend to be a little harsh in outline whereas the hackle tips give a softer, more gauzy appearance. The perfect winging material has yet to be found; hacklepoints have their faults, as when wet the fibres tend to cling together making the wing very slim indeed. Even with this fault they are more efficient than the normally used fibres taken from the primary feathers of such birds as the starling, coot or snipe.

Method of tying

Start very slightly behind the eye of the hook and carry the silk down to the bend; catch in three or four strands of bronze peacock herl and twirl them together to form a kind of fluffy rope effect. If the herl is to be wound in a clock-wise direction up the shank of the hook then the 'rope' turns should be anti-clockwise or they will come unwound. Wind the herl two-thirds of the way up the shank and tie in, trimming off the surplus. Take two white cock hackles and lay them together front (shiny side) to front, trim off the unwanted ends. Tie them in so that they slope back over the body in the fashion of a wet fly wing. Gently lift the wings into an upright position with your left hand and pass the silk behind them for a couple of turns; this will hold them upright. Now separate them and pass the silk in between making a figure-of-

Hacklepoint Coachman

eight binding. The more figure-of-eight turns you take the lower the wings should sit; I prefer the 'half' or 'semi-spent' position myself.

Take a ginger hackle – or two if the water the fly is to be used on is rather fast and rough – and trim off the fluff at the base of the feather. It is better to trim it with scissors as opposed to pulling the fibres off because this leaves a slightly serrated surface which the silk can grip. Tie in the hackle at the eye. Carry the tying silk behind and under the wings so that it lies hard up where the body of the fly finished. Wind a couple of turns in front of the wings, then pass the hackle behind them and wind on the remainder; tie in the point and carry the silk back to the eye. The silk must be kept very taut at this stage or it will push the hackle fibres out of true. Again the silk should pass under the wing. Whip-finish the head which should be as small as you can make it, and apply a coat or two of good-quality varnish.

I find that it helps the fish-taking potential of the fly if the hackle is trimmed off square underneath the fly so that it is just slightly longer at this point than the gape of the hook. I do this with most of my winged dry flies – it makes them sit lower in the water and therefore the trout does not have to stick his nose out quite so far to take them. The main advantage, though, is that nine times out of ten the fly alights in the upright position, not keeled over on one wing which is so often the case with untrimmed hackles. This must appear to be a much more natural position for a fly to float in than the lop-sided effect you would normally get. It has another advantage, albeit slight, that you can get away with using softer hackles because when the tips are trimmed off you reach a stiffer part of the fibre, and therefore the fly tends to float much better.

The Dressing

Tying Silk: Brown (Sherry Spinner)
Body: Bronze peacock herl
Wings: White cock hacklepoints
Hackle: Ginger or red cock
Hooks: 10 – 14 Old Numbers

WULFF PATTERNS

Lee Wulff, the American advocate of the minute rod called 'the Midge', invented some fly patterns which have been extremely effective both in the United Kingdom and in the land of their originator. The style of tying is not completely new, however;

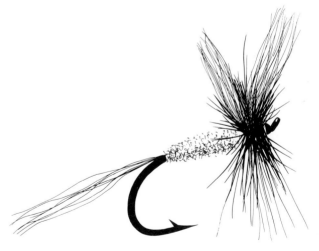

White Wulff

the Mole fly, for instance, used wings set on the fly in exactly the same way, and this was a popular trout pattern on my local river many years ago. Alas, the river Mole has now fallen far from its previous glory due to the building of the new town of Crawley and of Gatwick Airport. Lee Wulff uses hair-wings on his flies as opposed to feather, but the basic principle of the tying is virtually identical.

It is said that these flies were invented to imitate the mayfly and I have no doubt that this is so, but I have found they do much better in their smaller sizes. One memorable bag I made with the White Wulff was on the river Barle on Exmoor. It was an enormous pattern for this river – a size 10 no less – and the trout just could not get enough of it. The fish that rose to it were all very large indeed for this water where an extremely good average weight is two or three to the pound. These patterns catch fish on all types of water from the chalk streams of the soft southern valleys to the wild brooks of Exmoor and Wales. They have also accounted for several good catches on the reservoirs.

Method of tying
The standard Wulff dressings use mainly bucktail for the winging, but I have found that squirrel tail is generally more effective for

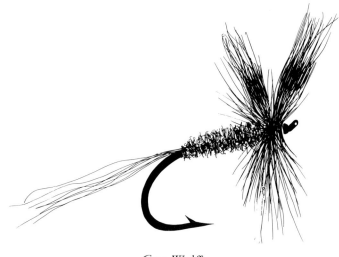

Grey Wulff

me if the appropriate colour is used. This is particularly so in the smaller sizes. I try on all my dry flies to match the tying silk colour to that of the hackle where this is possible; in the White Wulff for instance the hackle is badger (white with black centre stripe), therefore the silk is black so that it blends in.

Wind the silk down the shank and tie in a few strands of the winging material as whisks. Dub onto the silk some of the body fur and make a rough tapered body. Take this about two-thirds of the way up the hook shank. Now cut off a fairly large amount of squirrel tail hair and tie this in so that it points out over the hook's eye. Lift the fibres and wind several turns of silk under the hair round the hook shank, so that when the wing is released it is not lying flat along the hook but jutting up at an angle of about thirty or forty degrees. Divide this hair into two equal parts and make a figure-of-eight winding to hold the wings open.

Behind the wings tie in one or two hackles – I generally use two to aid flotation – from a good-quality cock cape. Carry the silk back to where the body finished and wind the hackle down to it, secure the tips with two or three tight turns of silk and complete with a whip-finish behind the hackle. It is essential on these flies to finish behind the hackle and not at the eye because the wings jut out over the eye and make the whip-finish very difficult indeed.

Royal Wulff

White Wulff

Tying Silk:	Black
Tail:	Fibres from a grey squirrel tail
Body:	Creamy white seal's fur
Wings:	As for tail
Hackle:	Badger cock
Hooks:	8 – 14 Old Numbers

Grey Wulff

Tying Silk:	Black
Tail:	Brown squirrel tail
Body:	Mole's fur
Wings:	As for tail
Hackle:	Blue-grey cock
Hooks:	8 – 14 Old Numbers

Royal Wulff

Tying Silk:	Brown (Sherry Spinner)
Tail:	Brown squirrel tail
Body:	Scarlet floss tipped at either end with peacock herl
Wings:	White hair from a grey squirrel tail
Hackle:	Ginger or light red cock
Hooks:	10 – 12 Old Numbers

GREENWELL'S GLORY

The dry-winged Greenwell is an excellent pattern on nearly all trout waters but as far as I am concerned it is first and foremost my favourite grayling fly. I have had some of my best catches of Test and Itchen grayling on this pattern. It seems to be effective even on the worst of days under the most miserable conditions. The fly was the inspiration of Canon William Greenwell and the first samples were tied for him by James Wright for use on the Tweed; the original tying was different from the accepted pattern of today inasmuch as it had no wire rib and the hackle was not of furnace cock but coch-y-bondhu; the wing was of blackbird's wing. The modern version is extremely effective, however, and in tests that I have done it proved to be better than the original

Greenwell's Glory (dry)

tying. I say this with apologies to the late Reverend gentleman. His one hundred and twenty year old invention has perhaps caught more fish for anglers throughout the world than any other single fly. He once said that his name would live on because of the fly he invented, and he was absolutely correct.

Method of tying

To start this fly you must first wax your tying silk well; primrose silk goes a translucent olive shade when waxed, and this is the colour you want. Wind the silk down the shank to the bend in close, touching turns, making certain that these turns do not overlap. Just before the bend of the hook starts, tie in the ribbing wire. Take the silk back up the shank over the first layer until you are within about a quarter of the hook's length away from the eye, rib the body evenly with the wire and make the turns fairly close together – about three wire widths between turns is correct. Trim off the spare end of the ribbing material. Tie in the winging slips; these are usually taken from a starling's primary feather. They can be tied in either as a single split wing or as a double if you really want to impress other anglers; I doubt if it will make the slightest difference to the fish!

A hackle is now chosen which shows a dark black list to the

centre of the feather. This is wound for two or three turns in front of the wings and then carried to the rear, and the remainder of the feather is wound. Finish in the normal way. This is another pattern where more than one hackle can be used to advantage if conditions demand it. Generally speaking, though, I prefer the single hackle because I like the appearance of lightly dressed flies, and I am convinced that the fish prefer them as well. The heavier dressing is an advantage for instance on a reservoir during a heavy 'chop' when there are some lake olive duns about, otherwise the fly can too easily be drowned.

The Dressing

Tying Silk:	Well waxed yellow or primrose silk
Rib:	Fine gold wire
Body:	Tying silk wound twice
Wing:	Starling's primary feather
Hackle:	Furnace cock
Hooks:	12 – 16 up eye, Old Numbers

WHITE-WINGED PHEASANT TAIL

This is one of my own patterns that was tied up on the spur of the moment one day, stuffed into a fly-box and forgotten until I was fishing a beat on the Hampshire Avon and could not find a fly that the trout wanted. I tied this on and looked at it as it floated down the river, liked the effect it created and then proceeded to take a limit of fish on it. It has since shown itself to be extremely good during that awkward time just before the 'evening rise' when the fish are not really keen on rising to anything. It is a good general pattern that I would not like to be without when fishing the chalk streams. I suppose you might call it a hybrid from the Hacklepoint Coachman and the Pheasant Tail; it is, however, very simple to tie and a very good fish-taker, especially in the smaller sizes.

Method of tying

Brown tying silk is run down the hook from eye to bend, there you catch in three or four fibres of cock pheasant centre tail, making them as deep a red as you can find. The tips are left

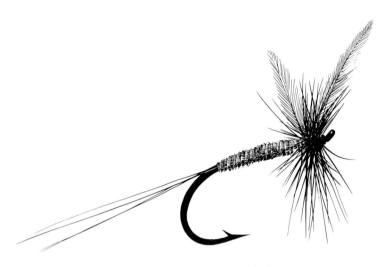

White-winged Pheasant Tail

protruding from the bend to make the whisks. I find it best on all my dry-fly tails to point them down as opposed to the more normal practice of taking a couple of turns of tying silk round the shank under the tail to make it cock up into the air. This is because I find it makes the fly float much better; the fly is then floating on two points of balance instead of the hackle on its own. It also lifts the hook-point above the surface film of the water which I believe makes the fly more attractive to the fish. At this stage of the tying I like to do something which Richard Walker recommends; this is to coat the hook shank with varnish and wind the pheasant tail fibres over this while it is still wet. This makes an extremely strong body which does not need to be ribbed, and so no extra weight is added to the fly. The pheasant tail is taken about two-thirds of the way up the hook, tied in and the end trimmed off. Two white hacklepoint wings are now tied in using exactly the same method as for the Hacklepoint Coachman.

The hackle is tied in and wound in the normal manner but on this fly I would never use more than one hackle. It wants to be as lightly dressed as you can make it. Make the whip finish at the eye of the hook.

The Dressing (see Plate 1)

Tying Silk:	Brown (Sherry Spinner)
Whisks:	Tips of body material
Body:	Cock pheasant centre tail wound over wet varnish
Wings:	White cock hackle tips
Hackle:	Ginger cock, one only
Hooks:	14–16 up eye, Old Numbers

BLACK GNAT

This fly is a rather difficult one to imitate because it is so small, rather like the *Caenis* in this respect. The one that I have found to be most effective is rather different from the normal patterns but my friends, clients and myself have all used it to good effect when these flies are on the water.

Method of tying

Black tying silk is wound from eye to bend, and a thin strip of dyed black-goose or swan feather is tied in, this is then wound half-way up the body over a coating of wet varnish as suggested for the previous fly. The surplus end is then cut off. A small wing of pale ginger hackle fibres is then tied to point over the eye of the hook in much the same manner as in the Wulff patterns except

Black Gnat

that in this case the wings are lifted into a more upright position before the fibres are separated. A very small black cock's hackle is then wound on. Whip finish behind the hackle, not at the eye.

The Dressing (see Plate 1)

Silk:	Black
Body:	Dyed black swan or goose
Wing:	Very pale ginger cock hackle fibres
Hackle:	Dyed or natural black cock, very small
Hooks:	16 – 18 up eye

DADDY-LONG-LEGS (CRANE-FLY)

While the crane-fly – or as I usually refer to it, the 'Daddy' – is not the most common food form for a trout to feed on, if these insects do manage to get themselves onto the water in any quantity and you have not a suitable imitation in your box, then you are liable to be in for a very lean time indeed. When the daddy-long-legs are about, the trout become completely obsessed with them, and this is very understandable; they represent quite a large mouthful for any fish.

My main experience with these insects is at Weirwood reservoir in Sussex; around about August or September they emerge in large numbers, and if the wind is blowing off the north bank a suitable artificial fished on the edge of the ripple can easily produce the biggest trout of the season. Like the mayfly and the big sedges they seem to bring out the bigger trout to feed on the surface, a rare experience indeed for these fish that normally browse along the bottom in search of caddis larvae, shrimps, snails and similar large food items. The larger a fish grows the more protein it requires in its diet and it looks for the place where these larger food forms are to be found.

I think that Dick Walker is correct when he says that to be at its most effective this artificial should merely be cast out and allowed to lie on the water surface without any retrieve being made. Daddy-long-legs are land insects and as such are out of place on the water; when they do get caught in the surface film their struggles quickly cease as they become waterlogged. I have many times risen fish to a dapped daddy-long-legs by just skimming it over the water surface but most of the fish have not taken the fly properly and were lost in consequence. Far better, I feel, to employ the normal floating fly line and cast the fly into the area of most activity and just leave it to sit there until that big old trout comes along and sticks his snout out for it! Always allow far more time for the fish to turn down than you would with most floating artificials, try to hold in your impatience to set the hook.

Method of tying

I am going to tell you about two methods of tying these flies; while basically similar, the tying that Richard Walker uses involves a long shank hook and a body material of cinnamon turkey tail. I much prefer to use those plastic mayfly bodies that are hollow and therefore float almost indefinitely without attention – they also allow the use of a much smaller hook which of course again aids the fly's floating potential.

Start the tying silk at the eye and run this down the shank to the bend, catch in several fibres of cinnamon turkey tail feather and wind these up the shank over wet varnish to a point about two-thirds of the way up the hook. Tie in and trim off the surplus. Now take individual strands of pheasant tail fibre and tie a single overhand knot in each, these are to simulate the legs and the

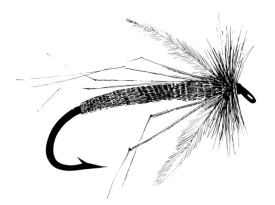

Walker's Daddy-long-legs

Collyer's Daddy-long-legs

knots are the 'knees'. Tie eight of these strands in this way and try to keep the knots the same distance from the tip of the fibre on all the legs. Tie the eight legs in, four on each side so that they trail 'astern'; do not put them on as they look on the natural fly on dry land, sticking out either side. Once the fly gets onto the water they seem always to trail their legs behind them. The wings consist of two gingery hacklepoint tips tied in the fully spent position so that they lie down well spread on the water surface. Two or more hackles are then wound on to give the fly good 'floatability'. This is the Walker pattern and it is quite as effective as the one I tie, but as always I prefer wherever I can to get the lightest effect possible on my flies and the hollow mayfly bodies help me to achieve this. My pattern differs in other respects from Dick's but not to any great degree.

Use a much smaller hook for my dressing, size 12 is quite large enough. Take the tying silk from the eye to about half-way down the shank, there you tie in a plastic mayfly body. These can be obtained quite easily from most fly-dressing specialists – they are shaped in the mould to make tying in easy and have a waisted effect; make certain that the turns of silk are very tight and that the plastic body sits directly on top of the hook shank.

The next thing is to tie in six legs exactly as in the first method. The wings I prefer are hackle tips taken from a light grizzle hackle, ginger barred with light red. The hackle is fairly sparse, four or five turns at most; it is the body that keeps it afloat, not the hackle. Whip-finish at the eye of the hook and coat the turns of tying silk at this point and also where the plastic body was tied in with varnish. This should help to prevent water seeping into the body.

The Dressings (see Plate 1)

Walker's Daddy-long-legs
Silk: Brown (Sherry Spinner)
Body: Cinnamon turkey tail
Legs: 8 cock pheasant centre tail fibres, knotted
Wings: Ginger hacklepoints
Hackle: Ginger cock
Hooks: 8 – 10 Long shank

Collyer's 'Daddy'
Silk: Brown (Sherry Spinner)
Body: Plastic mayfly body, hollow
Legs: 6 cock pheasant centre tail, knotted
Wings: Light grizzle cock
Hackle: Ginger cock, sparse
Hooks: 12 – 14 up eye Old Numbers

HACKLEPOINT MAYFLY

Unless you are fortunate enough to be able to go to Ireland or one of the other few unspoiled places of the world you are unlikely to see a really big mayfly hatch these days. Fifty or a hundred years ago the air above the chalk streams used to be a wavering haze of the big beautiful insects and the fish below grew fat and sleek on the abundance during those marvellous two or three weeks each year. How sadly things have changed: seepage from tarred roads, oil spillage and the constant washing into our rivers of inorganic fertilisers from the farms have slowly but surely reduced this annual feeding bonanza to a spectre of its former glory. A few rivers like the Test still manage to make reasonable showing, the Kennet is almost as good as it was, I have been told, but these famous and lovely rivers are not what they were.

For those who are still fortunate enough to experience a mayfly hatch of any sort I shall give the dressing of the fly which has taken more and bigger fish for me than any other mayfly pattern. This fly will certainly tempt the trout during their annual spree.

Method of tying
Wind the silk from the eye to the bend and tie in three strands of cock pheasant centre tail. These should protrude well out from the bend, about the length of the hook is right. Spread them out in a fan shape and slightly cock them upwards with a couple of turns of silk under the root of the tail. (This pattern is the one exception that I make to my normal practice of pointing the tail down.) Tie in your ribbing tinsel at this point as well, carry the silk back up the shank to the point a quarter of its length from the eye.

Now tie in a thin strip of natural raffia, about a sixteenth of an inch wide and a foot or so long. Take it down the body and up again, building up a neat carrot shape, smooth and tapering. Tie in at the point where you first started tying the raffia. Make a whip finish and cut off the silk. Now run a thin coat of varnish all over the raffia body and put the fly aside to dry. You can always be doing another tail and body while this takes place. Putting the

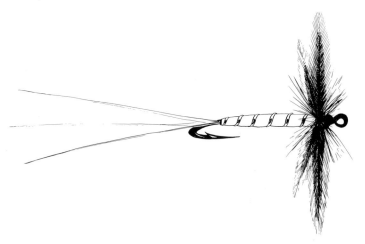

Hacklepoint Winged Mayfly

varnish over the body is most essential because raffia, being a natural vegetable material, retains a certain amount of moisture and consequently any ribbing put over it, if it contains a metal, will tarnish; the thin coat of varnish prevents this.

Rib the body of the now dry fly with even turns of tinsel up to where the body finishes. The wings consist of either one or two pairs of badger hacklepoints. If you decide to use two pairs then the rear two should be shorter than the forward pair, but whether there is really any advantage in double-winging is in my opinion debatable. Certainly from an aesthetic point of view they look far better but I have my doubts about whether the trout will appreciate your efforts any more than with the single pair of wings. I must say, though, that when I do demonstrations I always save this pattern to last and the 'customers' seem much more impressed with four wings than with two! It is best to tie all the wings in together if you use four feathers, rather than in two pairs; the space on the fly is limited and more turns of silk are needed if they are tied in separately. After the wing is tied and raised to the vertical position the two (or four) feathers are separated with turns of tying silk so that they lie in the fully spent position.

The hackle is tied in at the eye and wound for two or three turns in front of the wing, one turn in between the two pairs if four are used, and then finished off behind. The whip should be done at the eye of the fly.

PLATE I: Row I: Hacklepoint Coachman; Royal Wulff; Grey Wulff; White Wulff; Row II: Greenwell's Glory (dry); White-winged Pheasant Tail; Black Gnat; Walker's Daddy-long-legs; Row III: Collyer's Daddy-long-legs; Hacklepoint Mayfly; Lunn's Particular; March Brown (dry)

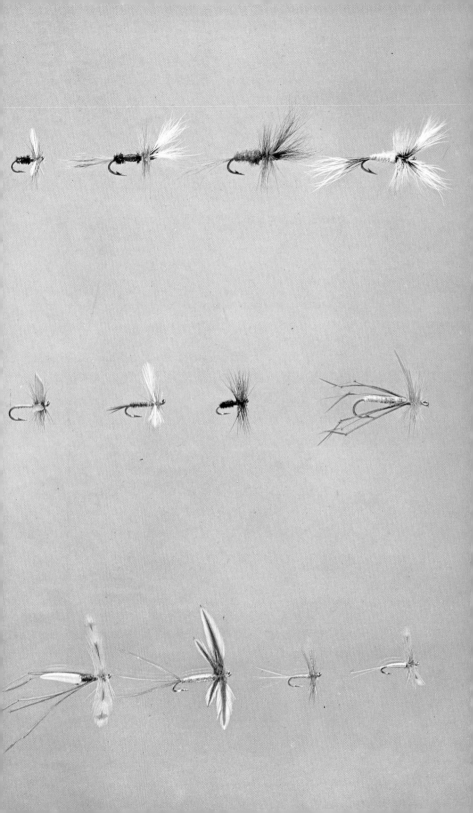

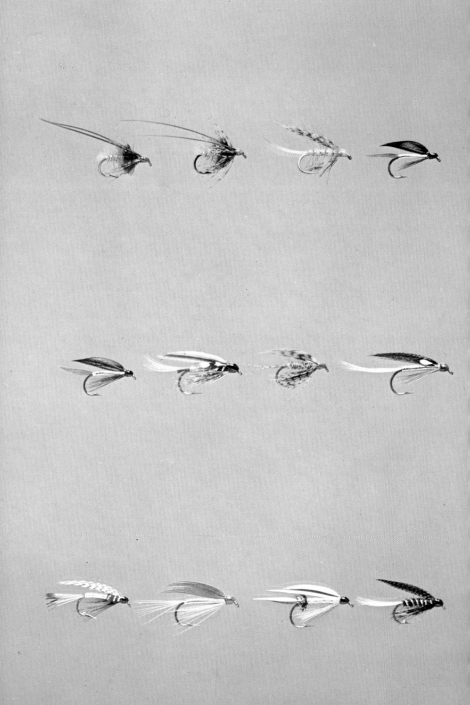

The Dressing (see Plate 1)

Silk: Olive or grey
Tail: Cock pheasant centre tail fibres
Rib: Oval gold tinsel
Body: Natural raffia, varnished
Wings: Two or four badger cock hackle tips
Hackle: Iron Blue cock
Hook: 10 long shank, up eye

LUNN'S PARTICULAR AND YELLOW BOY

Lunn's Particular is one of my favourite flies when there is a fall of olive spinners on any of the chalk streams. One of the nicest days fishing I have ever experienced was as the guest of Dermot Wilson on a stretch of the Itchen. During the early part of that day the only fly the fish would look at was the 'Particular', I must confess that later on I did get a couple of fish on a nymph when everything went rather dead but the bulk of my catch that day was made on Mr W. J. Lunn's fifty-year-old invention. It is pleasant to think that that tradition of river keeping has lasted through three generations on the famous Houghton Club water of the Test; that the name of Lunn still controls the most hallowed and exclusive fishery in the world.

The Yellow Boy has never been quite as popular as the Particular but I have found that I have never regretted finding a place

PLATE 4:   Row I: Walker's Longhorn Sedge Pupae (amber); Walker's Longhorn Sedge Pupae (green); Invicta; Bloody Butcher; Row II: Silver Butcher; Jock Scott (trout); March Brown (wet); Dunkeld; Row III: Peter Ross; Cinnamon and Gold; Parmachene Belle; Connemara Black for it in my box. Where there is a fall of the Pale Watery (*Baetis bioculatus*) it has always done well for me, particularly where the weed growth is very heavy.

Method of tying

Let us start with the Particular; fix your tying silk at the eye of the hook and take it in close turns to the bend, there you tie in the whisks. The hackle stalk body is also tied in at this point. This type of body gives a lovely ribbed effect without the necessity of using ribbing, thus avoiding making the fly heavy. This effect is achieved by stripping the fibres from each side of the hackle from a Rhode Island Red cockerel. Where the fibres are pulled off they leave the stalk creamy white but the remaining surfaces retain the red colour of the untouched feather. When this is wound onto the shank in even touching turns you get that marvellous ribbing effect. By using hackle stalks for the bodies on, his flies Mr Lunn also obtained another attractive feature; as the stalk is wound, the natural thickening of it makes certain that the body has a neat, smooth carrot-shaped taper to it.

The wings are applied in the same manner as those I have described previously, hacklepoints tied in the full spent position.

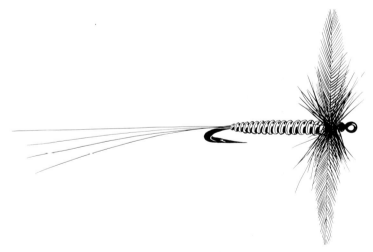

Lunn's Particular

After they are tied in, the hackle is wound in front and behind the wings and the whole thing is finished off at the eye.

The Lunn's Yellow Boy is tied in a similar manner but different-coloured materials are used, white hackle stalk dyed yellow for instance. We are indeed fortunate these days in having so readily available the various types of waterproof marking pens; these are obtainable in nearly any shade you need and are ideal for this type of work. Hold the stalk by the thick end over a piece of old newspaper on a table, press down with the felt tip of the marker and draw the stalk through. Do this a couple of times and you will have a perfectly dyed hackle stalk with none of the fuss or bother that is normally involved when dying materials. The marking ink dries in seconds when exposed to air. A marvellous invention for us flydressers.

The Dressings (see Plate 1)

Lunn's Particular

Silk	Crimson
Whisks:	Fibres of Rhode Island Red cock hackle
Body:	Undyed Rhode Island Red hackle stalk
Wings:	Medium blue dun hacklepoints
Hackle:	As for whisks
Hooks:	14 – 16 up eye

Lunn's Yellow Boy

Silk:	Orange
Whisks:	Buff cock hackle fibres
Body:	Yellow dyed hackle stalk
Wings:	Buff cock hacklepoints
Hackle:	Light buff cock
Hooks:	14 – 16 up eye

MARCH BROWN

This version of the March Brown comes from Australia and it has proved itself to be a good fish-taker, not merely on the rivers where this species hatch but surprisingly enough on such reservoirs as Blagdon, Chew Valley Lake and Eyebrook, mainly during their prolific evening rises.

There are many patterns of the March Brown. They come from all corners of the globe, some are excellent, others, alas, seem – to say the very least – dubious. They often have no resemblance whatsoever to any insect, let alone the March Brown with which we are familiar in this country. This pattern is, however, a very good fly to have about you, not just in March as the name implies but throughout the season; the same can be said of the wet-fly pattern which appears in the chapter on winged wet flies.

Through the use of white paint or varnish on the shank of this fly the floss-silk body assumes a beautiful translucent quality which is lacking from most artificial flies. This is really only apparent, though, once the fly has become dampened during fishing. It is certainly extremely pleasing to the human eye, and I believe it is equally so to a trout.

The hackles which are quoted in the dressing are for blue dun cock. All of the dun shades are extremely rare in their natural form; most of us therefore will have to make do with using dyed hackles. The substitutes seem just as effective but during the dying of any hackle some of the spring and resilience is lost. If you are forced to use dyed hackles on any dry fly, all you can do is grin and bear it and also be prepared to dry the fly more frequently.

Method of tying

Once again the tying silk is that light shade of brown called commercially 'Sherry Spinner'. Before we start to wind the silk we have to paint the hook shank with white paint or varnish; I much prefer the latter, as it dries much quicker and does an equally good job. After the coat of paint/varnish is well and truly dry, tie in the silk at the bend of the hook, and at the same point catch in your tail whisks. Carry the silk up the body for three-quarters of its length, making wide, open turns so that the white shank can give its full effect. Now tie in a pale honey-coloured floss silk strand. Take this down to the bend in smooth turns and then back up the body over the first layer, and fix and cut off the surplus at the point you first tied it in. Try to keep the body as thin as possible or you will not get that translucent effect you are after.

A wing of dark grizzle hacklepoints is now tied in using the

March Brown (dry)

semi spent position. Make quite certain they are at right angles to the hook shank and not pointing either forward or back, as that spoils the effect. Tie in a blue dun hackle close to the eye then carry the silk round behind the wings. Wind the hackle with an equal number of turns in front of the wings as you use behind them and secure the tip with two or three turns of silk. Trim off the hackle tip. Take the silk carefully through the hackle, remembering to keep it taut all the time, under the wings and finish at the eye with a neat, tight whip. One or two coats of varnish complete a fly which will take fish where no other fly will.

The Dressing (see Plate 1)

Silk: Brown (Sherry Spinner)
Tail: Three blue dun cock hackle fibres
Body: Pale honey-coloured floss silk
Wings: Dark grizzle cock hacklepoints
Hackle: Blue dun cock
Hooks: Painted white, 12 or 14 up eye

LAKE OLIVE

In my experience there are two of the olives with which the trout become obsessed when there is a big hatch, both at the dun and the spinner stage, and which are exceedingly difficult to imitate, the blue-winged olive and the lake olive. There is a theory that when seen from beneath both of these species exhibit a 'ruddy glow', a reddish colour that is not evident in reflected light. Be this as it may, there is no doubt that for me at any rate the pattern of lake olive I am describing here is far and away the most useful pattern I have ever found during a fall of these spinners. Strangely, it will also often be taken while the duns are on the water.

If you glance at the photograph you will see that it is a very peculiar 'olive' indeed – not a suggestion of olive anywhere on it. It is a very useful pattern used in conjunction with a nymph on the dropper. Even when there are thousands of olives floating on the surface and the fish are feeding quite happily on them, they will still take a nymph, as if a change of diet were welcome every now and again. I find it best to grease the leader and to treat the dry fly with a floatant of some kind leaving just the single dropper ungreased. A dropper length of between 5 and 8 inches seems to work best for me. The nymphs which I find most useful at these moments are my Green nymph or the American version of the Gold Ribbed Hare's Ear nymph.

The method of fishing is very simple. Find a good concentration of feeding fish, cast into the middle of them and then leave the fly to sit there; do not employ any retrieve but watch that dry fly like a hawk. If it so much as flickers then tighten: the nymph is being 'got at'. The dry fly itself will take as many fish as the nymph if not more, but which fly takes more fish seems to depend on which stage of the hatch you are fishing.

Method of tying

Start the silk very slightly back from the eye and wind down to the bend, just a shade round the bend is better. I much prefer the whisks tied in with the tail pointing slightly downwards. This allows two points of contact with the water surface and makes for a much better floater. Tie in half a dozen or so whisks, plus a length of fine gold wire. Wind the silk back up the shank binding down the spare ends of the whisks and wire as you go. Trim off any odd ends of wire and feather at the point where the wings will go and then carry the silk back down the shank to the tail

Lake Olive

again. Dub on some scarlet wool – very thinly – and wind a neat tapering body back up to the point where you trimmed off the spare end of wire and whisks. You will now need two nicely matched pale grizzle hacklepoints. Place them front to front (dull side out), the tips together. These points should be about three-quarters of the length of the hook shank; tie in the hacklepoints just as if you were tying in a wet fly wing – sloping back along the body. Remember that the dull side should be facing outwards at this point, quite the opposite to what you would want with a wet pattern. With your left hand gently lift the wings to a vertical position and take a couple of turns of silk behind the roots to make certain they stay that way. Separate the two wings and make sufficient figure-of-eight turns to hold them in the semi spent position, carrying the silk to the eye of the hook.

Finally, wind on a sparse hackle of light red or ginger cock. Finish winding the hackle behind the wings and secure the tip with three or so tight turns of the silk, trimming off the spare hackle end. You can now do a whip finish behind the wings; most fly-dressers seem to prefer to take the silk back to the eye of the hook and finish off in the usual way. I have yet to be convinced that if the job is properly done a winged dry fly is less strong if it is finished behind the wings; my own dry flies are usually finished in this way and they seem to perform just as well and last as long as those finished in the more conventional way at the eye.

The Dressing (see Plate 2)

Silk:	Brown (Sherry Spinner)
Whisks:	A few strands of ginger cock hackle
Rib:	Fine gold wire
Body:	Scarlet wool
Wings:	Light grizzle hacklepoints
Hackle:	Ginger or light red cock
Hook:	12 Old Numbers, up eye

CHAPTER TWO

HACKLED DRY FLIES

DARK TUP

The name of this fly is rather an anomaly, as any of you will realise who know the origin of the name 'Tup's Indispensable'. Tup is the old English name for ram, and no part of a ram's anatomy features in the Dark Tup. It is however rather similar in dressing to the Tup, varying only in the thorax colour. It is also rather like that famous West Country pattern, the Half Stone, except that the Half Stone is tied with a blue hackle and whisks whereas the Dark Tup uses honey hackles.

Successful as the Tup's Indispensable is – for me at any rate – the darker version does better. I have had some marvellous catches with this fly on waters varying from the chalk streams to that most lovely of our reservoirs, Blagdon. Like the Hacklepoint Coachman it is one of those flies that come into the category of 'old never-fail', well, rarely anyway!

This is one of the few dry flies I like to use as a 'high floater'. I do not trim the hackles on this pattern as I do on some of the winged flies. It must be admitted that there are occasions when the fish – the final result depends primarily on their mood of course – decide that a fly which floats well off the surface film is what they want. So the hackle fibres want to be fairly long and the tail whisks sloping well down to achieve this high float effect. I use the smaller sizes on the rivers, fourteens and sixteens, and reserve the bigger flies for use on the lakes and reservoirs. Not so much because the reservoir trout will not take the smaller size of fly but because if they do then they are much more likely to come adrift simply because they can be so big. No matter what some writers say, a big hook well set will always hold a fish better than a small one and on the big lakes the trout do not only grow very large, they are stocked that way. If you want to land the fish you hook then every part of your tackle needs to be in tip-top condition, but most of all the hook needs to be of reasonable dimensions and strong. While some rivers like the Test hold very large trout indeed, the average size of fish on most rivers is considerably below that of the stillwater fisheries.

Method of tying

Fix your hook in the vice and as you should always do, test it for temper, giving it a sharp tweak downwards with your forefinger tip, and also do the same thing in an upwards direction. As many people know to their cost if the hook is not tested upwards it is quite possible for it to break in a fish because the barb has been cut too deeply. It becomes an automatic reflex after a while to test hooks each time they are fixed in the vice, and a most important habit it is too. If there is any sign whatsoever of distortion, reject that hook, it is just not worth taking a risk with it, you will be let down at the vital moment as sure as fate.

Start the silk at the eye and run it down the shank to the bend; tie in half a dozen or so fibres of cock hackle, nice stiff ones, and take the silk up the shank, binding down the spare ends of the hackle fibre as you go. Go up the shank to about two-thirds of its

Dark Tup

length and tie in the floss silk. If two-strand floss is used it is most important that the strands should be separated and only one used; if you try to tie a smooth body with the floss as it comes off the spool you will find it virtually impossible, it always gets lumpy. Wind the floss down the shank to the bend and then come up the body again over the first layer getting a really smooth body and avoiding the ugly hump which results if the floss – or any material for that matter – is tied in at the tail. Tie in and trim at the same point where you tied in the floss in the first place.

Dub on a small quantity of mole's fur to the silk and wind this in front of the floss to form a spherical thorax; at this point make sure that you have not taken up too much room with the mole's fur; leave about a quarter of the hook's length clear towards the eye. Tie in your hackle by the thick end after having trimmed off the fluff at the base with scissors so that you achieve that serrated effect I mentioned in the previous chapter. Wind the hackle round the shank back towards the bend in tight even turns so the fibres stand out stiff and sharp at right angles to the hook shank, take a couple of turns of silk over the tip of the hackle to secure it and trim off the surplus feather. Finally, wind the silk back through the hackle, making sure you do not crush any of the fibres out of position en route. A neat whip finish and a spot of varnish completes a really killing pattern.

The Dressing (see Plate 2)

Silk:	Olive or Brown (Sherry Spinner)
Whisks:	Honey dun cock hackle, or very pale ginger
Body:	Lemon floss silk
Thorax:	Mole's fur
Hackle:	As for whisks
Hooks:	12 – 16 up eye

GREY DUSTER

The Grey Duster in its smaller sizes is as effective a pattern as I know during a hatch of *Caenis* (commonly known as the fisherman's curse because they are so difficult to imitate, due to their size), in fact I shall go so far as to say that it is really the only imitative pattern which seems to work at this time. The dressing of the Grey Duster that I use is a rather simplified version of the original, which involves whisks and a body of rabbit's grey under-fur. (Truth to be told, I ran out of rabbit fur one day when I was all set to drive to Wales the next morning, so I tied some up using mole fur instead, and the trout seemed to find them preferable.)

The 'Duster' is an absolutely marvellous pattern on fast mountain streams, and has proved a real blessing on most of my trips to fish that type of water. In the fast broken water it is one of the very few dry flies I know that are visible all the time.

When fishing on stillwaters during the *Caenis* hatch I find it pays to spot a rising fish – a regular riser with a definite beat, not a 'oncer' – work out its route and cast the fly to try and intercept it. This can involve quite a lot of time spent observing the fish before any cast is made. It is only too easy to put down a fish feeding on these small flies, particularly if you try to whack it on the nose with an artificial. It is far better to cast well ahead of him and hope that he will continue on the same route and fall into the waiting trap. It is also important that the fly should be left still on the water surface until he has travelled quite a distance, as a fish can easily be frightened by your withdrawing the fly from the water behind him. Another important point with this fly is that the rod should be very gentle. This is because the fly you are using is small and in consequence the leader point must be quite fine; I normally use about a 3lb b.s. point when using the Grey Duster. The loss of a certain number of fish is virtually inevitable when fishing fine on stillwaters but this loss can be reduced if the rod action is soft enough. Never 'strike' a fish when using this type of fly, either tighten gently or even do what I sometimes feel is necessary, and that is almost 'lean towards' the fish with the rod top and let the action of his taking the fly into his mouth draw in the small hook beyond the barb.

Method of tying

Nobody should find any difficulty in tying this fly, it is one of the simplest I know; care should be taken, though, that the body has a neat carrot-shaped taper to it, as it can make a difference.

Set your hook in the vice, just the bite of the hook, none of the

Grey Duster

bend, otherwise it is quite likely that you will damage the hook
if it is of the reversed type, and this will make it highly unreliable
in use by ruining the temper of the steel. Wind the tying silk
from slightly back of the eye to just before where the bend starts
in close touching turns. Dub on a little mole's fur to the silk and
spread this out as thinly as possible. Wind the dubbed silk from
the bend to about three-quarters of the way up the shank, making
that nicely tapered body as you go.

Take a well marked badger hackle and clip off the fluffy fibres
at the base of the stalk. For maximum visibility under bad conditions make certain that the white part of the feather is just that
and not pale cream. Tie in the hackle stalk, clip the hackle pliers
onto the tip of the feather and wind the hackle back in close turns
to where the body finished. Keep the silk really taut as you wind
it back to the eye of the hook where you finish as usual. Sometimes, particularly on the very small flies, I find it pays when
varnishing the head of dry flies to use three or four coats of really
thin varnish and allow this to soak into the hackle stalk and silk
by standing the fly 'on its tail' to dry, as it were.

The Dressing (see Plate 2)
Silk: Black
Body: Grey mole's fur
Hackle: Well marked badger cock
Hooks: 14 – 18 up eye, Old Numbers

COCH-Y-BONDHU

This is a most useful beetle imitation; the natural insect is found mainly in Wales (as the name indicates) and Scotland. Like the daddy-long-legs it is a land-bred insect that gets caught up in the surface film of the water occasionally. They can hatch in exceedingly large numbers at times, usually in the mid-season, and when this happens the trout go mad for it. Although the natural insect is rarely if ever found on English waters it is still a very good general pattern to have about you. Many anglers swear by it as the top dropper on a three-fly leader, however I prefer to fish it as a single fly in the normal dry-fly manner. It is mainly useful on stillwaters in my experience; I have never done very well with it on rivers other than in Wales when the natural insect was hatching in very large numbers.

Coch-y-bondhu

Method of tying

The tying silk is taken from eye to bend in the normal way and there a tag of gold tinsel or Lurex is tied in, two or three turns of fine tinsel (flat) are enough. Three or four strands of bronze peacock herl are fixed in just in front of the tag and these are wound up the shank in the usual way over wet varnish.

The hackle is the most important part of this fly. It should be well marked and the colour of the hackle should be clear and pronounced. The coch-y-bondhu hackle should be jet black in the centre, down the stalk, the middle of the fibres should be a good rich red and the tips of the fibres jet black again. The hackle is tied in by the stalk end and wound down to where the body is, there it is secured with turns of tying silk which is wound back through the hackle to the eye and finished off there. The hackle is best if it is wound fairly heavily, and to get this bushy effect it is usually better if two hackles are wound together.

The Dressing (see Plate 2)

Silk: Black
Tag: Flat gold tinsel or Lurex (fine)
Body: Strands of bronze peacock herl over wet varnish
Hackle: Coch-y-bondhu
Hooks: 12 or 14 up eye

IRON BLUE DUN

This is a small fly which is an absolute must if you are fishing chalk streams. The trout are very fond of it and they will often ignore other flies to pick off the odd Iron Blue coming down.

One day fishing on the Hampshire Avon with this pattern I startled both myself and the fish by taking the limit in under three-quarters of an hour; six casts, six fish. An interesting experience!

Method of tying

Run the tying silk from eye to bend and catch in two white hackle fibres as whisks, then tie in two strands of very dark heron herl taken from the secondary feather on the wing. Wind this up the

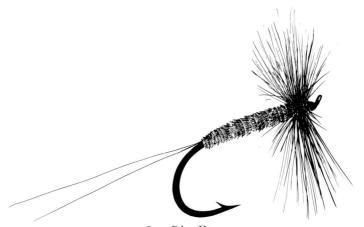

Iron Blue Dun

shank for three-quarters of its length over the wet, varnished shank. (Fly-dressers owe Dick Walker a vote of thanks for thinking of this very simple dodge. It makes the body of flies tied using feather fibre much more secure and lasting than anything else ever did; ribbing with tinsel was always a compromise between weight and security. Now if you want to, you can rib the body of flies tied over wet varnish with a contrasting single fibre of another feather to get the ribbed effect without being worried about whether it will float or not.) Tie in the heron herl and trim off the end.

PLATE 3:   Row I: Collyer's Grey Nymph; American GRHE Nymph; Water Tiger; Collyer's Shrimp; Row II: Walker's Leaded Shrimp; Mayfly Nymph; Phantom Larvae; Walker's Corixa; Row III: Polyethylene Corixa; Grey Midge Pupae; Buzzer Pupae; Walker's Midge Pupae

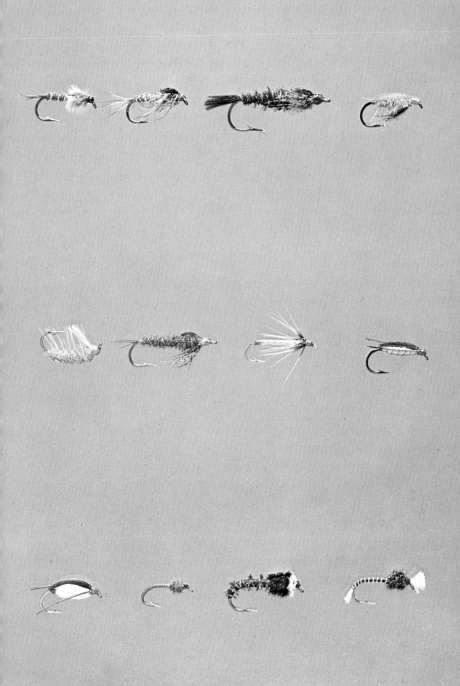

On many patterns of this fly a wing of starling dyed to a dark shade is used. I think that the wings are unnecessary and I do not bother with them on this particular fly. I tie in a hackle which is from as dark a blue dun cape as I can find.

The Dressing (see Plate 2)
Silk: Crimson
Whisks: Two white cock hackle fibres
Body: Dark heron herl
Hackle: Dark blue dun cock
Hook: 16 up eye

THE RED QUILL

This fly is probably one of the most reliable patterns for chalk streams, wild brooks or stillwater that are known. A favourite of the late F. M. Halford, it continues today along with its paler colleague, the ginger quill, to catch fish where all other flies fail. It is often tied in a winged version but I do not really think that wings are necessary; if you feel you must have them then use starling primary feather.

I well remember fishing at Eyebrook one day, and there was nothing doing whatsoever. The only fish I had seen was one that followed in a lure and then sheared off at the last minute. The sky was blue and the water was a flat calm; suddenly I heard

---

PLATE 2:   Row I: Lake Olive; Dark Tup; Grey Duster; Coch-y-bondhu; Row II: Iron Blue Dun; Red Quill; Walker's Sedge (1); Walker's Sedge (2); Row III: Shadow Mayfly; Great Red Sedge; Collyer's Brown Nymph; Collyer's Green Nymph

49

the sound of a reel turning fast. It was the chap in the next boat to me and he had a good fish on; after he had duly landed it and dispatched it I enquired what fly it had taken – 'A Red Quill', he replied. I found this rather strange because his next cast was obviously on a sinking line and he stripped it in as if he were in a hurry to get home. Obviously the Red Quill is a far more versatile fly than I had hitherto given it credit for being . . .

Method of tying
Brown tying silk is carried down the shank to the bend where the tail whisks and the body material are tied in. This body material is of stripped peacock herl and I have found that by far the easiest way of stripping the flue off the stalk is to use an ordinary soft eraser, such as is used for pencil marks, and rub the stalk against the grain while resting it on a hard, smooth surface. The best quill to use for the body is one that shows a distinct dark and light stripe. These are usually the fibres taken from the 'eye' feather.

After the whisks and the stalk are tied in I like to build up a slightly tapering body with tying silk, the taper stopping about three-quarters of the way up the shank. The silk taper is then

Red Quill

coated with a thin layer of varnish and the stalk wound over it and tied off where the taper on the silk ends. A bright red cock's hackle is then wound on and finished as usual. The Ginger Quill I use is tied in exactly the same manner except that the whisks and hackle are of ginger, not red, and the peacock herl is of as light a shade as I can find.

The Dressing (see Plate 2)

Silk: Brown (Sherry Spinner)
Whisks: Red cock
Body: Built up with tying silk, covered with well marked stripped peacock herl
Hackle: Bright red cock
Hook: 14 – 16 up eye, Old Numbers

CHAPTER THREE

SEDGES

WALKER'S SEDGE

This fly is one of the 'wake' flies: it is tied in such a way as to create a disturbance on the surface of the water as it is retrieved. All the flies in this chapter fall into this category but this one was invented by Richard Walker specifically with this fishing action in mind. It stands up on its hackles as it is retrieved, and the pulls of the retrieve want to be fairly fast. There is a considerable amount of skill involved in judging just what is the speed at which a trout will be most likely to take these flies; it comes either with trial and error on the day or through years of experience.

I thoroughly enjoy using sedges on stillwaters; the beauty of them is that you see all the action. A fish moves, perhaps twenty yards from you, you make your cast and the fly lands six or eight feet in front of him. You start the retrieve immediately and the long stiff hackles make a heavy wake; the fish turns towards this disturbance, probably curious, then as he sees the fly he comes after it, his back breaking the water surface. You must not speed up or, even worse, slow down the pulls of line with your left hand but keep the fly moving steadily and sooner or later you will feel the hard pull as the fish catches up. Never, ever, strike until you feel that pull, otherwise all you will succeed in doing is pulling the fly straight out of his mouth and scaring him. If you find the suspense unbearable then shut your eyes – yes, literally, shut your eyes – until you feel the fish. It is only too easy to strike too soon, believe me, I know . . .

Method of tying
There are two different methods of tying this fly, and I shall give them both, to save any confusion. The first one which Dick

52

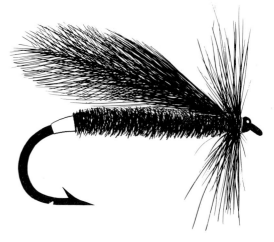

Walker's Sedge (1)

used went as follows: the tying silk was taken from the eye to the bend and then a piece of fluorescent orange floss silk was tied in, this was wound as a fairly long tag. Three or four strands of chestnut-dyed ostrich plume were tied in and twisted together and then wound over wet varnish for about two-thirds of the long-shanked hook's length. With a pair of sharp scissors the flue on the body was then trimmed off so that the stalk showed clearly through. The scissors must be held absolutely flat along the hook for this job to be done satisfactorily.

The wings consisted of a pair of furnace cock hackle tips tied in back to back to lie low along the shank like a normal wet-fly wing. These were tied in rather long and the tips then trimmed with scissors to give a nice rounded shape. The hackles were of two long-fibred red cock hackles tied in together and wound together to give quite a thick, bushy effect just back from the eye.

The latest – and I think, improved – version of the Walker Sedge uses an ordinary-length hook, size 10 seems best, and after the silk is wound down the shank a small amount of fluorescent orange wool is either wound in as a strand or dubbed onto the silk and wound as a very short tag. Several fibres from a cock pheasant's centre tail are then tied in and again wound up the hook over wet varnish. This material is short in the flue and in

Walker's Sedge (2)

consequence there is no need to trim off the flue as there is with the earlier pattern. A choice of winging material can be used on this fly, either a bunch of hackle fibres from a red cockerel which are trimmed off square about the length of the hook, or you can use fibres from a cock pheasant centre tail treated in the same manner. Either wing should be tied so that it lies low along the back of the fly. This pattern also looks rather attractive if the wing of furnace hackles back to back is used, as in the first dressing. The hackles are again red cock tied in rather longer than they would be for most dry flies.

The Dressings (see Plate 2)

Walker's Sedge 1

Silk:	Brown (Sherry Spinner)
Tag:	Fluorescent orange floss
Body:	Ostrich herl (chestnut) trimmed after winding
Wings:	Furnace cock hackles back to back, and tips trimmed round
Hackle:	Two red cock hackles, long in fibre
Hook:	8 long shank, Old Numbers

Walker's Sedge 2

Silk:	Brown (Sherry Spinner)

Tag: Fluorescent orange wool
Body: Cock pheasant centre tail
Wings: Bunch of red cock hackles or cock pheasant centre tail
         fibres, tips trimmed square
Hackle: Two red cock hackles
Hook: 10 – 12 up eye

PETER DEANE'S SHADOW MAYFLY

The Shadow Mayfly was originally invented as just that, a may-fly. Peter tells me that it is most effective in that capacity, but it also makes a lovely sedge pattern, which is what we are primarily concerned with here. A long-shank hook is used and the silk is wound from the eye to the bend, where a few fibres of Plymouth Rock hackle are tied in. The tip of another Plymouth Rock cock hackle is also tied in at this point and wound in close, touching turns up the shank. When you reach the end of the hackle, tie in and trim off the surplus feather, repeat the procedure with another hackle. Keep winding hackles until you reach a point roughly a third of the shank's length from the eye. There, wings of two ginger cock hackles are tied in back to back, and the ends are trimmed off as in the first version of Walker's Sedge. Another hackle is now wound in front of the wings.

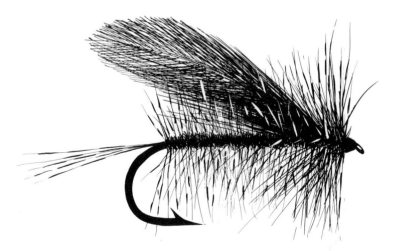

Shadow Mayfly

Some years ago Peter told me that he always trimmed off the hackles flat underneath on this pattern, as in fact I do on a lot of my winged dry flies. If you cannot get Plymouth Rock hackles, then I have found that a suitable substitute is any really stiff light-coloured grizzle hackle. The beauty of this dressing is that it floats almost indefinitely without any treatment from a floatant. It only has to support the weight of the hook because there is no body as such and no rib.

The Dressing (see Plate 2)
Silk: Black
Whisks: Plymouth Rock cock hackle or grizzle cock
Body hackle: As above
Wings: Ginger cock hackles trimmed round at the tips
Throat: As for whisks
Hooks: 12 – 8 long shank

THE GREAT RED SEDGE

This fly is a standard pattern that has survived the years and catches many fish for people. I well remember one evening fishing a beat on the Hampshire Avon. The limit was a modest one brace of sizeable trout but although I had been really trying during the day all I could catch was a few small, out-of-condition grayling. The light was going off the water and a fish started to rise opposite me. He was making slashing takes at something scuttering across the surface; sedges.

I hastily tied on a size 12 Great Red Sedge (a size smaller than is normal for this fly) and made my cast. The fly landed about a yard above his last rise; I let the fast centre-of-the-river current catch the line and it drew the fly across in front of him making a wide, heavy wake. The fish came at it and – missed. Another cast to the same spot and again he rose, this time the hook went home and he took off up that river going as if he would never stop, three, four, five jumps and then a fast turn, and he tore off downstream of me, the reel was screeching and I had to run down the bank to keep up with him. Eventually he was landed, a lovely rainbow of slightly under two pounds. By this time the light had virtually gone but as I walked back upstream what should I see but another fish moving in precisely the same place as the first; I shall not bore you with a repeat of the above story which was almost exactly what happened again, except that this one did not miss on his first rise. But it just goes to prove two points: the first is that sedges are very handy patterns to have with you, and the second is that it pays very often to stay on the banks until the last moment, or at least until the rules say that you must leave. A day which had produced nothing worth talking about earlier on had left me with a lasting memory and two fine fish that I should otherwise have never caught.

Method of tying
Fix your hook into your vice and give a couple of test twangs, starting the tying silk slightly back from the eye, wind it down the shank to the bend and catch in several fibres of stiff dark red cock's hackle, at the same time tying in a length of gold wire. Dub on some mole's fur and run a fairly thick but tapered body to about two-thirds of the way up the hook.

Where the body ends tie in a red cock's hackle and wind this palmer-fashion down to the tail, then secure it by ribbing in the

Great Red Sedge

opposite direction with the wire. Tie off and trim where the hackle was tied in. Tie in a wing of brown speckled hen primary feather so that it lies low over the body; make it just as you would a wet-fly wing. In front of the wing tie in another cock hackle and wind this from the eye down to the front of the wing; there you secure the tip with turns of tying silk. Carry the silk through the hackle to the eye, being careful not to crush any fibres out of place, and make a neat whip finish.

The Dressing (see Plate 2)

Silk:	Brown (Sherry Spinner)
Whisks:	Red cock hackle
Rib:	Gold wire
Body:	Grey mole's fur
Body hackle:	Dark red cock
Wings:	Brown speckled hen's wing
Throat:	Dark red cock's hackle
Hooks:	6 – 10 up eye, Old Numbers

NYMPHS, LARVAE, PUPAE AND CORIXIDS

CHAPTER FOUR

NYMPHS

COLLYER SERIES OF NYMPHS

Originally I tied just three patterns in this series, or rather coloured variations of the same pattern – the basic construction is virtually identical in all three – green, brown and black. I have since found that the black tying is nowhere near as useful as the others, so I have dropped it. Of the other two the green is by far the most popular with my fly-dressing clients. Since those early days I have tried various different combinations of colours, grey, red and black, blue dun, claret and a hot-orange version. Of these the grey and the blue dun have had the best results for me. The grey nymph proved to be by far the most spectacular of all these patterns inasmuch as it has now accounted for the largest rainbow trout ever taken on a fly in the United Kingdom. This was a splendid fish of 9lb 12oz taken by Norman Fance from Dermot Wilson's Nether Wallop pool down in Hampshire.

There has been a lot written in recent years in the angling press about these giant fish from tiny lakes; in case you might be misled into thinking that the fishing on these 'ponds' is easy, let me straight away dispel that illusion. Any decent fish that was taken from Dermot's pool at any rate, came out the hard way. I have fished it several times and my biggest fish so far is a rainbow that weighed in at 6lb 8oz. Although by any standards that is a pretty big fish, it should be borne in mind that every single cast was covering fish as large and in some cases much larger; I am hesitant to say that there are 12lb rainbows in there, but some of them must certainly be very close to that weight.

These nymphs were originally tied because I was dissatisfied with the existing patterns that were available, and I decided to try and create something better. I was not trying to make an 'exact' copy of the natural; what I wanted was a caricature, a fly to suggest just one thing to the trout – food, good, safe, edible food. I dragged a plankton net around Weir Wood reservoir towing it behind a boat wherever I saw fish feeding on nymphs – a wicked thing to do, I know, but justifiable in this case, I feel! When I returned home I copied some of the nymphs I found. Not only did my customers approve of the results, the trout did too. What I wanted was a general representation of a food form, and in these patterns I appear to have hit the right combination. I have had letters from people as far away as Peru and Tasmania telling me that the nymphs have been effective with local fish. In Britain they have taken trout from Caithness to Cornwall in all types of water. They were invented primarily for use on reservoirs but they can be equally good in running water.

These Collyer-type nymphs are very easy to tie but it is quite a different matter to make them look exactly right. For instance, although I call one of them a 'green' nymph, it is not green at all, it is olive. I have seen some dreadful examples of 'Collyer's Green Nymphs' that were a beautiful shade of emerald; the colour they should be is a pale washed-out olive. The beauty of these flies is that the colour variations can be tremendous even though the tyer is sticking to the same style of dressing throughout. I hope that you will experiment with colour variations of your own and see what your particular 'fancies' can accomplish. As I said earlier, without any shadow of doubt the 'green' nymph has proved by far the best fish-taker for most people – of course as usual I must be awkward and say that my favourite is the brown one!

Method of tying

Wind the tying silk from the eye to the bend and catch in several fibres of the body material, leaving the tips sticking out as a tail. Do not, repeat do not, trim them to the right length, tie them in correctly in the first place. The tail should be about half as long as the hook length. Now tie in the ribbing tinsel. Wind the feather fibres to half-way up the shank and secure firmly with the tying silk so that the waste part of the feather sticks straight up-wards. Rib the body carefully with neat, evenly spaced turns of tinsel (four or five turns are ample), secure at the point where you

Collyer Nymphs

tied in the feathers of the body.

A piece of ostrich plume is now tied in so that the flue faces back towards the tail; wind it in very close turns to within about a sixteenth of an inch from the eye. Tie in with the silk and trim off the surplus. With the left hand gently part the ostrich flue on the top of the hook and bring the butt of the body material over and through the flue so that it lies snugly along the shank, tie in at the head and cut off the waste. Whip-finish the head and apply a coat or two of varnish.

The Dressings (see Plate 2)

Collyer's Green Nymph

Silk:	Olive
Rib:	Oval gold tinsel
Body:	Olive goose or swan
Thorax:	Olive-dyed ostrich herl
Hook:	10 down eye, Old Numbers

Collyer's Brown Nymph

Silk:	Brown (Sherry Spinner)
Rib:	Oval gold tinsel
Body:	Cock pheasant centre tail
Thorax:	Chestnut-dyed ostrich herl
Hooks:	10 – 12 down eye

Collyer's Grey Nymph *(see Plate 3)*

Silk: Black
Rib: Oval silver tinsel
Body: Undyed heron primary feather
Thorax: Natural undyed hen ostrich herl, badger colour
Hook: 10 down eye, Old Numbers

AMERICAN GOLD RIBBED HARE'S EAR NYMPH (GRHE)

As far as I am concerned the name of this fly is an anomaly – rather like that of the Dark Tup. When I dress this pattern I do not use fur from the hare's ear at all; it is the body hair I use. This may sound like sheer sacrilege to any of the 'old school' of fly-dressers reading this, maybe, but it is eminently practical. The hair which can be obtained from a hare's ear has two short-comings, one, that there is not very much of it, not in the right shade anyway, and, two, that if you want to tease out the hair for a hackle effect it is too short to do this properly. I remember that when I first started tying flies I sat for hours puzzling how to get fibres that were at most a quarter of an inch long to stretch to make a hackle that would support a dry fly on the surface of the water. Nobody ever tells you that the longer fibres have to be taken from the body of the animal. I was quite frustrated for a while, until I finally realised that everybody cheated anyway! It just goes to prove that you should not take anything at face value in this life – I'm sure that little episode turned me into the cynic I am today . . .

This fly is certainly one of today's fly-fishing success stories. In all the reports I hear they say that it's 'a real killer on this water' or 'old so-and-so told me he had his limit at Two Lakes in the morning on it', and so it goes on. I first saw the dressing in the American magazine *Field and Stream* about 1968, I thought it looked pretty likely and tied some up. My next trip was to Darwell reservoir in Sussex and I went out in the boat and came in very quickly indeed with a limit bag of six fish. The thing I like about this fly is that it is a good fish-taker at all depths. The fish at Darwell were taken fairly deep down, I was using a forward taper sink-tip line and letting it go down for a minute or more before I started the retrieve. On another occasion at Chew

I was taking fish off the top during an evening rise of buzzers – it is versatile, as I said. The *Field and Stream* tying of it called for a long-shanked hook but after I had tied a few like that I did not like the look of them too much and decided to try a normal-length wide-gape hook; as Dick Walker would say 'Much more betterer it were!'

Method of tying

Wind the tying silk from eye to bend in the usual way and catch in some straight fibres of hare's body hair, a bunch of a dozen or so about half the hook-length long. A piece of gold oval tinsel is tied in at the same point – for the smaller flies I use gold wire. Some hare's body fur is now dubbed onto the silk and wound to form a carrot-shaped body, take this about half-way up the shank. Rib with the tinsel, even, tight turns, remember. Trim off the spare end of ribbing material.

A strip of dyed black turkey tail is now tied in, about an eighth of an inch wide, shiny side upwards. The strip should lie along the body and point towards the tail. Now dub some longish fur on the silk and wind a fairly thick thorax. In this instance it is best if the hair is dubbed onto the silk quite heavily because when it is picked out with the dubbing needle the more turns of silk you have the more likely you are to pick up that silk with the needle's point. Carry the turkey tail fibres over the thorax and tie in. Finish the head and varnish.

After the varnish has dried, pick up the fly again and tease out some of the fibres of the thorax with your dubbing needle to

American GRHE Nymph

make a 'hackle'. In this pattern, I think you will find, you have a real killer.

The Dressing (see Plate 3)

Silk:	Brown or black
Tail:	Hare's body hair
Rib:	Oval gold tinsel
Body:	As for tail
Wing cases:	Dyed black turkey tail
Thorax:	Long fibres of hare's body hair
Hooks:	10 – 14 down eye

THE WATER TIGER

Several autopsies I have performed on trout taken from southern counties reservoirs revealed large and (due mainly to the digestive processes) unidentifiable insects. Call them nymphs if you like, but they were far bigger than the normal run of nymphs, all of an inch and a quarter long. Dragonfly larvae, I thought, and left it at that; then I found one that the fish had obviously only recently swallowed. It was intact and it proved to be the Water Tiger, larva of the Great Diving Beetle *Dytiscus marginalis*. It obviously makes an excellent mouthful for any trout, and I decided to make an artificial which would resemble (if vaguely) the creature.

To get a 'nymph' of this size would necessitate using at least a size 4 long-shank hook and, to say the very least, this would look incongruous; it also seems to be unnecessary because the dressing on a size 10 long shank or at most a size 8 gives the desired effect, and taking the tail into account it then makes a pretty fair representation of the natural.

The Water Tiger is an extremely aggressive creature which will not hesitate to attack small fish. I remember well as a child when I went on newt-catching expeditions it was quite common to feel your fingers being nipped by the little brutes. They seem to frequent mainly the shallow water of lakes and ponds near to weed-beds, and this is where the artificial should be fished to be most effective. The adult beetle rises to the surface every now and again to take in air but the larvae are mainly bottom-dwelling creatures, and because of this the imitation should be fished deep. The retrieve should be of short pulls with a lengthy pause in between.

Method of tying

This pattern is fairly complicated and does raise a few problems for the dresser but they are not insurmountable. Fix your long-shanked hook in the vice and give it a good testing for temper. Carry light brown tying silk down the shank to the bend and there tie in a strip of sepia condor herl and a length of copper wire. The tip of the condor herl is used to make the tail so let it stick out past the bend a quarter of an inch or so. Wind the condor herl up the shank, building up a slightly tapering body to a point about two-thirds of the way up the shank, tie in. A single strand of bronze peacock herl is now tied in and wound down the body in the opposite direction to that taken by the condor strip. This is then ribbed by the copper, again travelling in the opposite direction to the peacock herl. Tie in the copper wire where the condor ended and trim off. This ribbing will hold the delicate peacock herl really firmly.

In front of the body you dub on a fairly bold thorax of yellow/olive seal's fur or wool. Take this to within about an eighth of an inch from the eye. Carry the surplus end of the condor herl over the thorax, tie in at the eye and trim off the end.

If your vice has a head that swivels it is a help at this stage because you now tie in a few strands of brown partridge hackle

Water Tiger

each side of the head. These are tied in in exactly the same way that a beard hackle is tied in on a wet fly except that they are each side, not underneath. If you prefer it, you can always wind the hackle in and divide it with an over and under figure-of-eight binding. It is much neater, though, if you use the beard or false-hackle system.

The Dressing (see Plate 3)

Silk:	Brown (Sherry Spinner)
Tail:	Tip of body material
Rib:	Copper wire
Gills:	Bronze peacock herl
Body:	Sepia condor herl (pale)
Thorax:	Yellow/olive wool or seal's fur
Wing cases:	End of body material
Side Hackles:	Brown partridge
Hooks:	8 – 10 long shank

COLLYER'S SHRIMP

I call this fly my 'shrimp', but like the series of Collyer nymphs it is not intended to be a close imitation of the natural freshwater shrimp, merely a representation of a shrimp-like form of life which looks good to eat – from a fish's point of view, that is. The trout seem to find it acceptable as such, and this after all is our prime objective. I should like to make it clear, by the way, that I do realise that shrimps swim on their backs while this little beastie does not, but if the trout are not so particular, who am I to argue?

I tie three variations of the Shrimp and they all seem to be equally effective in the right circumstances. The backs and in one case the ribbing are the only things that vary.

Method of tying

Wind olive or light brown tying silk down the shank and stop just before the start of the bend and there tie in a strip of olive goose, cock pheasant centre tail or heron primary feather – the same feathers, you will notice, that are used in my nymph series. This strip should hang off the end of the hook, shiny side (bad

Collyer's Shrimp

side) upwards. Catch in at the same point the ribbing material. Dub on a body that tapers fore and aft, from the short hairs right at the root of a grey squirrel's tail, where it joins the body of the animal. It always helps if you shoot the squirrel yourself and cut off the tail to the right length because the long guard hairs farther up the tail are hopeless and most commercially supplied tails are cut off too short. Rib the body neatly up to the eye and trim off the surplus. Bring the feather fibres over the body and tie in at the head. Reverse the fly in the vice and tie in a false hackle of brown partridge back feather, spread it out well so that it does not hang as a 'lump' underneath. Whip-finish the head and varnish.

The Dressing (see Plate 3)

Silk:	Olive or light brown (Sherry Spinner)
Back:	Olive goose, heron primary or cock pheasant centre tail
Rib:	Fluorescent magenta floss or gold wire
Body:	Hair from the base of a grey squirrel's tail
Hook:	10 down eye, Old Numbers

WALKER'S LEADED SHRIMP

In the same letter in which Dick Walker sent me the dressings of his Longhorn Pupae he also included the tying for this 'fly', I know that he has used it with great success, not only for trout but also for grayling on the chalk streams. It is a little difficult to get the dressings completely right but it is an excellent pattern once this has been achieved. As I said when discussing the Collyer

69

Shrimps, these creatures swim on their backs, and this fly is designed specifically with this swimming action in mind, hence the heavily leaded back of the artificial.

Fly-dressers have tried for years to get a really good imitation of the freshwater shrimp, and this is certainly the nearest that anyone has come to it; they are very difficult animals indeed to create out of fur, feather and tinsel but they do form a quite large proportion of a fish's food and are consequently of considerable importance to the fly-angler.

Method of tying
Wind the silk from the eye to the bend of the hook and catch in the tip of a ginger cock hackle. Carry the silk back up the shank again and bind in a strip of lead foil, take this lead backwards and forwards along the top of the hook shank tying it down with the silk as you go; five layers are needed. This should give the characteristic 'hump' to the back of the fly that is so noticeable in the natural; it also ensures that the artificial swims on its back. This means of course that the hook point is far less likely to foul any debris on the lake or river bed.

After the lead is firmly secured tie in at the eye a strand of wool, olive or olive-brown would be best; wind this down to the bend then up over the first layer to the eye again. It would probably make a neater job if the wool were to be dubbed on the silk and wound from the bend to the eye. It might depend, though, on how neatly the lead foil was tied in: you may need quite a

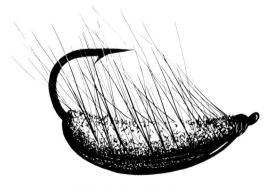

Walker's Leaded Shrimp

thick layer of wool to cover up any unevenness. The silk must end up at the head one way or the other.

Clip your hackle pliers onto the butt of the 'ribbing' hackle – it was left hanging off the bend, remember? Wind the hackle palmer-fashion up the body and tie in and trim at the eye. Very carefully trim off all the fibres of hackle except those on the under-side of the fly. Take the fly out of the vice and drench the back in varnish, keep doing this until it is smooth and shiny.

The Dressing (see Plate 3)
Silk: Brown (Sherry Spinner)
Body: Wool, over five layers of lead foil bound onto the back of the hook shank
Hackle: Long cock hackle (ginger) wound palmer-wise, clipped off on the back and the sides
Back: A thorough soaking in cellulose varnish to produce a smooth back
Hooks: 10 – 12 Old Numbers

MAYFLY NYMPH

The Mayfly Nymph is sometimes a useful pattern to have about you but generally speaking it is far less effective than a good floating fly; certainly this is true on a day when there is a big mayfly hatch on a river. You may pick up an odd fish or two before the fish start feeding in earnest on the duns but once that stage of the proceedings is reached there is very little hope of interesting a trout in anything below the surface. I find, though, that these flies make an excellent nymph for use on our stillwater fisheries – even those which have never seen a mayfly. I imagine the trout take them for dragonfly or damsel fly larvae but what-ever the explanation might be – they do take them.

Method of tying
I use an olive tying silk for this fly and take this down the shank from the eye in open turns to the bend. Tie in three strands of cock pheasant centre tail as whisks – they want to be fairly short, say a quarter of an inch long; tie in at the same point a piece of gold wire. Now mix some olive and brown seal's fur together

Mayfly Nymph

and dubbing this onto the silk, wind it about two-thirds of the way up the shank. Run the ribbing tinsel up to the same point and tie in and trim off the end.

A strip of hen pheasant tail feather is now tied in, the dark part, leaving it shiny side up and pointing towards the tail as with the black turkey in the G.R.H.E. dressing. Dub in a fairly thick thorax of seal's fur, about twice as thick as the carrot-shaped body; bring the pheasant feather over the top of the thorax and tie in at the eye, trimming off the spare end. Now reverse the fly in the vice and tie in a false or beard hackle of grey partridge breast feather, whip-finish, varnish the head, and that's it. Lots of books tell you to apply varnish with a brush, but it is far better in my opinion to put it on the heads of flies using the tip of the dubbing needle; this is stiff and allows you to apply the varnish with precision.

The Dressing (see Plate 3)

Silk:	Olive
Tail:	Three short strands of cock pheasant centre tail fibres
Rib:	Gold wire
Body:	Mixed olive and brown seal's fur
Wing cases:	Dark hen pheasant tail
Legs:	Grey partridge breast feather
Hook:	10 long shank, Old Numbers

CHAPTER FIVE

PHANTOM LARVAE

One day a couple of years ago I had an invitation from Alex Behrendt to have a try for his fish at the beautiful fishery of Two Lakes in Hampshire. Alex said he had 'a little problem' that might interest me. He wanted me to try and fashion an imitation of a creature that has baffled fly-dressers for years, the phantom larva. Now how do you set about trying to copy a creature which is virtually invisible? It is no easy-task. I sat at his table with my vice set up and my travelling fly-dressing kit spread out in front of me and thought about the problem for several minutes. What I needed was a starting point. Then it came – of course, polythene. That would be fine for the body material; now to size, shape and action. After several false starts I arrived at a number 12 round-bend hook, olive tying silk, stretched polythene and a badger hackle.

I tied in the silk at the bend of the hook – the initial fixing was fairly wide, about six turns of silk, to make the dark blob at the tail end of the natural. The silk was then wound in open turns up the shank to the eye where the polythene strip was tied in. The best width for this seems to be about one-sixteenth of an inch. The polythene was then carefully taken down the hook and slightly round the bend so that it overlapped the dark patch. It was then spiralled smoothly back up the shank to the eye. I found that to get the effect I wanted, thickness of body and transparency, two layers was the maximum. The polythene was then tied in and the surplus cut off. The hackle did not need much thinking about – it had to be a fairly long-fibred, soft badger, tied in to slope back over the body. A couple of turns were enough. I wanted the bulk of the hackle's length to be virtually invisible, hence the white outer fibre, but at the same time I wanted the pronounced dark patch at the head which is so

73

Phantom Larva

obvious on the natural, and a badger hackle filled the bill exactly.

When I returned home I tied up a dozen or so to this pattern for dispatch to Alex so that some of his rods could give it a trial; but looking at them I was not completely satisfied, something was missing. After study I decided that it was the body, it just did not give enough appearance of transparency. The bronzed hook would have to go. I looked through my hook collection for inspiration and there, nestling in a corner of a compartment were a few silvered hooks. I fished them out; they were size 14 long shank and when I measured them against the natural they matched up even better than the size 12 I had been using.

As soon as I had tied the first fly I knew the silvered hook had been the missing factor; the finished fly looked far more lifelike than the patterns tied on the bronze hooks. I made up a dozen of the new type and sent these along for testing as well as the first batch. Within the week a letter arrived with a Romsey postmark and it revealed that we had hit the jackpot. Alex and his clients were delighted with the results the new fly had given. It has one big advantage over most 'nymph-type' patterns – it can be fished at almost any depth and still be effective. It also seems to take fish in the most adverse weather conditions.

You will find when dressing the Phantom Larvae that the silk will slip badly on the silvered hooks unless it has been well waxed. I am no lover of wax – in fact I hate the mucky stuff – in this case it is necessary, however. Try to keep the body slim and transparent and use as little hackle as you can – it is there only to give the fly a little 'life' and to provide those tiny fish-attracting vibrations as it is drawn through the water.

The Dressing (see Plate 3)

Silk: Olive
Body: Stretched polythene
Hackle: Badger (hen or soft cock)
Hook: 14 silvered long shank

CHAPTER SIX

CORIXIDS

WALKER'S CORIXA

I should think that in the last few years Dick Walker has invented more really useful fly patterns for the stillwater angler than anybody else in Britain. If he says a fly will catch trout, you can be sure it will; so it is with his corixa dressings. Of course no fly has ever been invented – nor ever will be – that will take trout under any conditions or in all circumstances. All fly-dressers search for such a fly but if it is ever found then we professional tyers will all be out of business – I am not really too worried about it though . . .

All the many and various corixa tyings have caught fish, but I have never been too happy with most of them and I have found the Walker dressings to be the best. The 'paddles' make them look very like the natural, this gives me confidence, and *that* catches fish. Dick's original tyings had olive (pale) floss silk bodies. To please a big customer I tied them up with a white body and then compared the two by fishing with them: the white won.

Method of tying
Wind the tying silk from the eye not quite to the bend of the hook, and tie in the tip of the feather strip to be used for the back and the paddles, and leave it hanging off the back of the hook, shiny side (inside) up. Catch in the ribbing tinsel and take the silk back almost to the eye, where the floss silk is tied in and wound up and down the shank to form a sausage shape. Tie in at the eye and cut off the surplus.

Rib the body evenly with four or five turns of the ribbing tinsel, tie off and trim. Now bring the back feather over the body to the eye, pull it tightly and tie in. With a dubbing needle separate the two outside fibres of the back material, then cut out the

Walker's Corixa

middle section with scissors, and trim it off close to the silk. Bend the two long outside fibres back along the body and tie down at the head so that they retain their position – at an angle of about thirty degrees from the body.

With the left hand hold the two paddle fibres together and trim them off just behind the hook. If the paddles are not held together you will find that it is very difficult to make them the same length. It is a bit like trying to trim off pieces from a chair leg to get it to sit evenly on the floor – you end up with very short legs. Whip-finish the head and apply two or three coats of varnish.

The Dressings (see Plate 3)

Olive-backed Corixa

Silk:	Olive
Back:	Olive dyed turkey tail
Rib:	Gold wire
Body:	White or olive floss
Hook:	12 Old Numbers

Brown-backed Corixa

Silk:	Light brown (Sherry Spinner)
Back:	Cock pheasant centre tail
Rib:	Gold wire
Body:	White or olive floss
Hook:	10 Old Numbers

POLYETHYLENE (PLASTAZOTE) CORIXA

This pattern is what you might call a joint effort; about 1969 Dick Walker invented the buoyant-bodied Rasputin using a polyethylene body, I looked at it, liked the idea and then the thought came into my mind 'Why not a corixa with a similar body?' It would seem, though, that at about the same time someone else had that thought, R. D. Bradbury up in Cheshire (our illustrator). This was all completely unknown to me at the time; I wrote an article about this type of fly for my column in *Angling* about six months before that article was due for publication – the Editor likes to plan well in advance! I was quite surprised and amused when just the month before my article was due to come out there was one by Derek Bradbury on the self-same subject, saying almost exactly what I was going to say a month later. I can see how he might have thought the idea was stolen from him – it was not, it was pure coincidence that we both happened to have the same though at about the same time. As I said, a 'joint effort'.

To fish this fly to its best advantage a sinking line must be used. The corixa patterns, or water-boatmen if you prefer, always seem to do best if they are fished in the vicinity of weed-beds, therefore the shallower water – up to about 12 feet deep – will be the best place. The fly is cast out and the line is allowed to settle right on the bottom; the leader should be long enough that it can reach from the bottom of the lake right to the surface. The fly is then retrieved by using long slow pulls of line with long pauses in between. This allows the fly to swim down for three or four feet and then drift back up to the surface again, just as the natural does when it is collecting air. A leader-strength at the point of not less than 5lb b.s. should be used because the takes when they come can be extremely vicious. The takes seem to occur usually when the fly first starts its downward movement. I can only think of a couple of occasions when the fly was taken as its great bouyancy carried it back up to the surface. This business of the really violent take is rather peculiar; I have found over the years that this usually happens only when imitative flies are used, normally nymph patterns are the prime example. I have been smashed on the take several times when nymph-fishing but very rarely indeed if I have been using a lure of some kind. I am inclined to believe that this is because the trout has to pursue the lure at a fairly high speed and the impetus thus created carries the fish onwards towards the angler and softens the pull felt at the rod. With nymphs the fish is cruising perhaps at right angles to the line and the nymph is just taken 'in passing' as it were, hence the solid thump. Funny, though; you would think it would be the other way round.

Method of tying

The back feather is tied in in exactly the same manner as the Walker patterns but after this is done you make a whip finish to hold the silk in place and cut the tying silk off. A piece of poly-ethylene foam or better still the closer grained plastazote is then cut off and trimmed roughly to shape with scissors. A needle is heated with a match and passed longitudinally down the piece of foam. It goes through very easily and care has to be taken that the hole is central; the body is then trimmed exactly to shape. Derek Bradbury brought out a very good point in his article; the foam plastic is so very buoyant that you must be certain that the bulk of the body shape lies above the hook shank otherwise the fly will swim on its back.

A coating of varnish or thin adhesive is now applied to the hook shank and the body is eased onto the hook from the eye. This is a pretty elastic material and provided the hole was made

Polyethylene (plastazote) Corixa

by a heated needle – this melts the inside surface of the foam and makes sure the hole stays open – there should be no real problem. The tying silk is then re-tied to the eye end of the hook, and a few turns of silk are taken over the very tip of the body to secure it in place until the adhesive dries. The back and the paddles are treated in precisely the same manner as on the Walker flies, and the head is finished off in the same way.

The Dressing (see Plate 3)

Silk: Brown or olive
Back: Olive or brown feather fibre
Body: Expanded polyethylene or plastazote
Hooks: 10 – 12 down eye, Old Numbers

CHAPTER SEVEN

PUPAE

GREY MIDGE PUPAE

The midge pupae patterns are the ones which are, as far as I am concerned anyway, fished slower than any other. The method I use is this; I watch the lake surface for those tiny sipping rises – these are most easily seen where there is a calm area of water, and they are easily mistaken for small fry or coarse fish, only experience can tell you the difference. Mind you, even after many years it is still only too easy to be fooled.

The midge pupae patterns are best fished on a knotless taper leader going down to a point of about three to four pounds' breaking strain. This is greased right up to the fly (it may even prove worthwhile to put a little silicone floatant on the thorax of the fly). This will ensure that the pupa floats right in the surface film with its hooked tail hanging downwards just as the natural does before emerging.

If any retrieve is employed at all it should be extremely slow – more of a twitch to the line every ten or fifteen seconds than a retrieve as such. At most the line should be drawn half an inch or so with a long, long pause between the tiny movements. It will be found that even on the calmest of days there is a certain amount of surface drift and this usually gives quite sufficient movement to the fly without any retrieve. What should be avoided if possible is that large bow in the line caused by the faintest breath of air, as this will move the artificial at far too great a speed. Seek out the flatest, calmest conditions you can find.

When a fish takes it will normally be a very gentle sipping rise. Now control yourself! Don't strike! Pause for a second or so and then very gently feel for the fish, the action of the fish turning down will be quite enough to set the small hook; a strike will usually only result in a break of the leader. Play the fish gently.

I have had trout of over 4lb by this method on points as light as 2lb b.s. A soft-actioned built-cane rod is a great help in softening the shock to the leader, but whatever rod you use, be gentle.

Method of tying
The Grey Midge Pupa is really a very simple fly to tie; all you need in the way of materials is a strand from the eye feather of a peacock's tail, some mole's fur, black tying silk and some small hooks.

Wind the silk from the eye to half-way round the bend of the

Grey Midge Pupae

hook in close turns; take it well round the bend and make certain the turns of silk are close-butted to one another. The strand of eye feather now has to be stripped of its flue, and this can be done in one of three ways: you can draw it through your forefinger and thumb, pressing hard with the nails of both, drawing it against the grain as it were. Or it can be laid on a smooth, hard surface and the flue scraped off with a razor blade; the last, and I think the best method by far, is again to lay it on a smooth surface and rub it with a soft eraser, the type you would use to rub out pencil marks; it must be a soft one, though. This last method takes off the flue fibres quickly and cleanly with far less danger of damaging the quill. There is another method which I have tried – with a remarkable lack of success, I might say – and that is to soak a bundle of the eye feather fibres in a weak solution of bleach. It takes off the flue all right, but the snag is that it also makes the quill extremely brittle. The timing of the dipping is very critical, and the rinsing has to be very thorough indeed. However, I expect that with practice it could be quite a good method, and it does have the advantage that large quantities of quill can be stripped at the one time.

Tie in the thin end of the quill where the silk ends and again wind the silk in close turns to within a quarter of the hook's length from the eye of the hook. Wind the quill over the silk in close-butted turns to the same position; this gives a splendid 'ribbed' effect to the body because of the light and dark shading of the stripped quill. The next thing is to dub on a small quantity of grey mole's fur which is then wound to make a round, ball-shaped thorax. Finish at the eye and make the head as small and neat as possible.

The Dressing (see Plate 3)

Silk: Black
Body: Stripped peacock herl
Thorax: Mole's fur
Hooks: 14 – 18 down eye, Old Numbers

BUZZER PUPAE

Buzzers or chironomids are the very large bumbling flies that one sees over stillwater, usually in the late evening. They are very easy to identify because of their markedly hooked abdomen; the back end curls round in a very pronounced manner. They always look slightly sinister to me; they seem as if they ought to carry some potent stinging mechanism in that hook, but luckily for the angler they are completely harmless. The trout feed extensively on both the larvae and the pupae, more so the latter because they are more easily available to the trout at this stage of their development. I have never been sure whether or not the trout take the hatched fly, certainly no imitation of the flying insect that I have ever used has proved successful. The form of a trout's rise to the buzzer pupae is easy to identify, it is a slow, lazy head-and-tail rise, usually repeated many times and fairly close together. This pattern of rises allows the angler to position his fly well to intercept the trout on its 'beat'.

There are two basic methods of fishing these pupae, and both seem equally useful depending on the stage that the hatch has reached. The first method is to search the water with a sunken fly or a team of two or three. The flies are cast out and allowed to sink under their own weight; a floating line is far and away the best for this. A fair amount of time should be allowed for them to get down five or six feet, the line is then pulled in long, slow draws of a couple of feet or so. When the flies reach the surface they are allowed to sink again and the pattern of the retrieve is repeated until the cast is fished out. Takes can be extremely savage so care should be taken that you are not smashed as the fish takes the fly. I rarely use a leader that is less than 5 lb b.s. for these flies for that reason. Buzzers usually hatch over the deeper water and it can sometimes pay to use a really long leader – say fifteen to eighteen feet – and try this method of retrieve but allow a far longer sinking time. The best way by far of judging a fly's depth either using the long-leader method or with a sinking line, is to time the sink from the moment you cast on the second hand of your watch. It may well take two or three minutes for the flies to sink to the depth at which the trout are feeding.

The second method which I have found useful is to watch for cruising fish and to cast four or five yards in front of them. When I judge they are getting close to the flies I gently tweak the line a few times to give the pupa a semblance of life and movement. The takes on the surface are usually nowhere near as hard as the deep-down takes.

Method of tying
The silk is carried from the eye right round the bend of the hook and there a piece of either copper, gold or silver wire is tied in. The silk is now wound back up the shank for three-quarters of its length and a piece of floss silk of the appropriate colour is

Buzzer Pupae

tied in. The floss is wound down the shank to the point where the ribbing wire was tied in and then carried back up the shank and tied in and trimmed at the place it was first fixed. It is best, I find, if the second layer of silk is made to taper from the tail to the front of the abdomen. A strand of peacock herl with flue as short as possible is now fixed by the butt end and wound down the body in wide, open turns. This is fixed into place by winding the wire up the shank in the opposite spiral and tying in where the herl started. The wire and the tip of the herl are then trimmed off. A bold thorax of three or four turns of chenille is then wound; make certain you leave a little room at the eye because the next step is to wind two turns of white ostrich herl in front of the thorax. Make a neat head and the fly is finished.

The Dressing (see Plate 3)

Silk:	Black, brown or olive
Rib:	Copper, silver or gold wire
Body:	Black, scarlet, orange, claret, brown or olive floss
Gills:	Short-fibred peacock herl
Thorax:	Chenille to match body colour
Front:	White ostrich herl
Hooks:	6 – 12 Old Numbers

WALKER'S MIDGE PUPAE

Once again the name of Walker comes up: Dick ties some very effective midge pupae patterns, which are much more lightly dressed than my buzzers and make a good intermediate pattern between the tiny Collyer Grey Midge Pupae and the much more bulky buzzer patterns.

They have the advantage that they are relatively easy to tie, and they are very useful flies to have in one's box. They are slow-sinking and so are especially useful if fished in or just below the surface film.

Method of tying

Tie in the silk a short way back from the eye of the hook and as soon as this is done tie in a bunch of white cock hackle fibres so that they point butt forwards. Carry the tying silk down the shank and slightly round the bend in close-butted turns. The ribbing material is tied in at this point and a thin skim of varnish is run up the silk already wound down the shank. A second layer of silk is then wound over the first in close turns again and once more a coat of varnish is run onto the silk. Before this has a chance to dry the body is ribbed; carry the ribbing about three-quarters of the way up the shank, tie in and trim off the surplus. Tie in strands of the thorax material, carry the silk up to where the bunch of hackle fibres was tied in, again run varnish over the turns of silk, twist the thorax fibres to form a rope effect and

Walker's Midge Pupae

wind these over the wet varnish to form a neat thorax. Trim off the ends. Make a few turns of silk in front of the hackle fibres to lift them up slightly, make a whip finish and varnish. The white 'breathing tubes' should be trimmed off fairly short.

To make this pattern sink even slower you can tie in a bunch of squirrel hair behind the thorax to give the impression of a hatching midge. Dick says that the best colour for this bunch of hair is black; I must say that for me at any rate the best colour has come from a brown squirrel tail. The sinking rate on these flies slows down also if the ribbing material is white hackle stalk rather than tinsel in one of its various forms. I must say, though, that on one occasion at Eyebrook reservoir I did very well by using one of Dick's midges but tied up with a narrow silver Lurex rib. I tried the more standard types but the trout just were not interested; I was surprised that something as small as the different types of ribbing material could affect the results obtained to such a marked degree.

The Dressing (see Plate 3)

Silk:	Black, brown, olive or orange
Breathing Tubes:	White cock hackle fibres, trimmed
Rib:	White hackle stalk, fine silver flat Lurex or oval tinsel
Body:	Tying silk or floss to match
Thorax:	Peacock herl, dyed swan or sepia turkey
'Wing':	Black or brown squirrel tail fibres
Hooks:	10 – 18 Old Numbers

WALKER'S LONGHORNS, GREEN AND AMBER
SEDGE PUPAE

I have received the dressings for these two patterns only very recently. Consequently I have had no opportunity to try them out, but Dick tells me they're taking fish 'all over' and that, as they say, 'can't be bad'. They are pretty easy to tie and they have that certain 'feel' to them; I am certain they will take a lot of trout on the reservoirs. They also fill quite a big gap in the stillwater man's fly patterns; there are very few patterns indeed that are tied up specifically to imitate sedge pupae. I think the only one that comes near it is the Stick Fly which is supposed to look like the caddis larva in its case, but certainly there are no pupae patterns aside from these – that I have come across anyway, with Dr Bell's Amber Nymph as a possible exception. (The Stick Fly is usually tied on a long-shank hook, about size 10. The body is thin and made of wound peacock herl; at the head there are a couple of turns of short ginger cock hackle to simulate the legs.)

Walker's Longhorns

John Goddard in his book *Trout Flies of Stillwater* lists one dressing of a sedge pupa but it is not of the Longhorn type.

I should like to quote a passage from Dick Walker's letter to me in which he sent both the dressings and a sample of these flies and one of his Leaded Shrimp, the dressing of which was given earlier. 'The Longhorns I consider a most valuable addition to the range of stillwater flies. They have been successful on every lake and reservoir I have fished, often outstandingly so. The number 14 green is doing very well at Grafham just now.'

Method of tying
Carry the appropriate-coloured tying silk from the eye to the bend of the hook and catch in a length of the ribbing tinsel. Take three or four strands of either green or amber ostrich herl and tie in the tips, run varnish up the shank of the hook. Twist the strands of ostrich herl together to form a rope effect and wind this up the body for two-thirds of its length; tie in and trim off the ends. Rib the rear portion with the tinsel. Tie in three or four strands of sepia-dyed ostrich herl and wind this in a similar way towards the eye of the hook, leaving a small gap behind the eye; again the ostrich is wound over wet varnish. Tie in and trim. Wind a hackle of brown partridge back feather in front of the body. This should be tied in such a way that it slopes back over the ostrich herl.

Take two strands of pheasant tail fibre and tie these in at the eye so that they also slope back over the body; separate these two fibres. They should be about twice as long as the hook. Wind a neat head, whip-finish and apply two coats of varnish.

The Dressing (see Plate 4)
Silk: Brown or olive
Body: Rear two-thirds; green or amber ostrich herl, twisted and wound thick, ribbed with fine gold thread. Front third; sepia ostrich herl
Hackle: Brown partridge
Horns: Two strands of pheasant tail fibre, twice as long as the hook
Hooks: 10 – 14 Old Numbers

SECTION THREE

WET FLIES

CHAPTER EIGHT

WINGED WET FLIES

INVICTA

There are certain flies which although extremely popular with most anglers have never achieved results for me, namely Mallard and Claret, Dunkeld, and the Black and Peacock Spider. Until very recently the Invicta also fell into this category, but a couple of seasons ago I was forced to change my mind – for the first time I started catching fish on it.

It is a most peculiar thing, the fact that some fly-fishermen use certain patterns which take fish for them but which prove to be completely useless in the hands of another man. Take the Peter Ross for instance; I have had probably more fish on that single pattern than on any other but the number of people I have spoken to who said they found it completely hopeless is legion. Ken Sinfoil, the head bailiff at Weir Wood reservoir was responsible for persuading me really to try the Invicta; apparently the trout were being extremely difficult at this particular time, and he said that the only fly which was consistently taking them was this pattern. I thought the least I could do was to humour the poor demented fellow! I said I would tie one on the point of the leader and keep it there all morning, come what may.

I rowed the boat out over the deep water by the dam; the day was a flat calm and no fish were moving so I decided that a slow sinking line was probably the best bet. My cast went out, the line settled through the surface film and began to sink. After about ten seconds everything went tight and I found I was play-ing a nice brownie of about a pound and a half; he had taken the Invicta 'on the drop'. I had several more fish that day and they were all on the same fly. Since then I have used it fairly ex-tensively during similar flat calm conditions, and usually it manages to take a fish or two. The reason for this peculiar business

of a fly working for one man and not another can, I think, be
accounted for in two possible ways. The man who finds a fly
effective is possibly moving it in a different way from the man
who enjoys no success with it. The other reason, I think, is –
confidence. You make a killing with one particular fly, and,
without your realising it, it becomes a favourite and spends
much more time on your leader than would a fly which has yet to
prove itself. It is a truism that you cannot catch fish on a fly unless
you are using it.

I should feel happier about fishing the Invicta if I could fathom
just what the fish take it for; people say it looks like a sedge; so
it does but have you ever seen a fully winged sedge swimming
about submerged? I doubt it. Again I am told it could represent
a hatching sedge when fished just sub-surface, and once again I
am forced to agree that yes, it could, but perhaps somebody
could now explain to me just why it catches fish at all depths,
because I cannot work it out. But catch fish it undoubtedly does
and that is what this book is primarily concerned with, giving
the angler flies which really do take trout, and not merely per-
petuating folklore or plugging someone's particular 'fancies'.

Method of tying

Start winding the silk at the eye of the hook and when you reach
the bend, tie in a golden pheasant crest feather; the ribbing tinsel
is caught in at this point as well. To make certain these materials
are really firmly fixed carry the silk up the shank over the spare
ends and then back down to the tail again. A quantity of either
wool or seal's fur is now dubbed onto the silk and this is wound
up the shank to form a slightly tapering body. The dubbing
should finish about a quarter of the hook's length from the eye.
A cock's hackle is now tied in by the stalk end – since this is a
wet fly a softer hackle can be used than would be the case for a
dry pattern. It is a good opportunity to use up any of the 'B'
quality capes you might have, without affecting the fly's performance. The hackle pliers are then clipped onto the tip of the hackle
and this is palmered down the body to the tail. The ribbing tinsel
is then carried up the body, through the hackle, taking the opposite spiral to that taken by the feather, the hackle stalk is thus

held firmly in position. The tinsel is then tied in at the same point where the hackle stalk was.

The fly is now reversed in the vice and a false hackle is tied in under the throat. At this stage I should perhaps explain my reasons for using 'false' or 'beard' hackles for most of my winged wet flies. The main reasoning behind this is that if the hackle stalk is wound behind the eye, and carried under the fly with the silk, there is an unavoidable bulge created that will throw the wings high up, and I much prefer a sleek, narrow, low-lying wing, because I think that, tied in this way, they catch more fish.

Invicta

There is of course a way to avoid this effect and still use wound and divided hackles, which is to build up the turns of tying silk in front of the stalk until they are completely level with it. This has the unfortunate tendency to make the head far too large and bulky. You then end up with a lumpy, ugly fly that certainly would not inspire confidence in me, and I have always felt that confidence on the angler's part is half the battle in taking fish. From a professional fly-dresser's point of view there is another distinct advantage to false hackles; this method enables him to use all the cape, not just the feathers that happen to fit the size of the hooks.

All that you do to tie in a false hackle is to put the hook into the vice upside down and taking one or perhaps two (if you want a bulkier effect) of the bigger hackles at the base of the cape and holding them together you tear off a bunch of fibres; these fibres are then held in your left hand and measured against the hook length and then trimmed to length *before* they are tied in – by doing it this way rather than tying in first and then trimming you avoid the possibility of any 'stumps' of fibre sticking out under the head. It is possible that with a little practice in this method you can spread the fibres with your left thumb as the silk goes round them so that you get a soft silhouette instead of a hard lump hanging under the hook. When this is done by an expert it is virtually impossible to tell a fly tied this way from a wound hackle except of course that the wing sits on the fly so much better.

With the material we are using to tie this particular fly you can drive yourself mad trying to follow various instructions for splitting the stalk and winding the jay's hackle in; believe me, I know! It is so very much simpler to tear off the required amount of hackle and fix it in as a false hackle under the throat of the fly, and as you are going to have trouble with the winging of this fly anyway it seems to me rather foolish to make things even more difficult by putting that 'hump' under the wings to throw them out of true.

The fly is now put back the right way up in the vice and the wings are tied in. The wings are made of two strips of hen pheasant centre tail. This is quite a difficult feather to work with because the strips taper so much. The answer I have found is to tear off strips about a quarter of an inch wide; this gives you at least a small amount of bulk and you should get quite a reasonable wing. People try to get round this winging problem by substituting hen pheasant wing feather for the tail, but this just does not look the same, and to get the correct appearance to the fly the wing must be from the tail feather.

I have not tried it yet myself but at the 1972 Draycote press day Dick Walker's wife Pat had a nice brownie on an Invicta tied up with a scarlet tail. I believe red ibis substitute feathers were used; it might be worth a try some time.

The Dressing (see Plate 4)

Silk: Olive
Tail: Golden pheasant crest
Rib: Gold oval tinsel
Body: Yellow wool or seal's fur
Hackle: Ginger cock
Throat: Blue jay
Wing: Hen pheasant centre tail
Hooks: 8 – 14 Old Numbers

SILVER AND BLOODY BUTCHER

These two flies are good old 'standards' for stillwater fishing. They take fish on most of the British reservoirs and in their smaller sizes are extremely popular in Scotland on the lochs. Generally they are fished as part of a team of flies, and their position on the cast is almost invariably as the 'point' fly. They are said to resemble a small fish in appearance as is the Peter Ross; if I want to imitate small fish I feel there are better patterns such as the Sinfoil's Fry or the Polystickle but certainly they do take fish for many people.

There is not much doubt that the Silver version is by far the most popular and I cannot quite make out why this should be. I think that my results have been fairly evenly matched between the two flies. The only difference after all is that the Bloody Butcher has a scarlet hackle instead of a black one.

Method of tying

When I wrote about this fly in my column in the magazine *Angling,* there was a considerable fuss made about the fact that I recommended the tying silk should be carried down the shank of the hook in open turns, not, as is normal, close-butted.

The point about winding open turns of silk down a hook when tying this type of fly is that so often one sees flies which have lost their tail because it pulled out. This is particularly true of the Butcher patterns when the tail is fixed in by just a few turns of silk at the bend of the hook and the remainder is trimmed off. By winding open turns of silk and then tying the tail in, if the spare ends of the tail strips are then bound down on the top of the

Butcher

hook shank by other turns of silk this crushes those fibres into the lower layer and makes the tail completely immovable; I have even tried to pull the tail out with a pair of pliers, and all that happens is that the tail breaks off at the junction with the body of the fly. The two layers of silk make an intermeshing serration that really grips the fibres and holds them in place. The second layer of silk over the first plus the crushed fibres fill in the interstices and the whole thing is virtually as smooth as if the body were made of close turns of silk in the first place.

Another point I should like to make here is that so very often the tail on a Butcher points off to the side. This is because the dyed duck feathers used to make the tail have a pronounced curve to them. The best way of avoiding this curve is to tie in two sections of fibre much as you would for a wing; the two opposite curves act against each other and you end up with a perfectly straight tail. The two strips are of course tied in 'upside down', pointing in the opposite direction to that taken by my normal style of winging.

After the tail is tied in satisfactorily, carry the silk up to the point a shade behind the eye (binding down the spare end of the tail fibres as you go) and catch in a piece of either flat tinsel or Lurex. I prefer Lurex myself because it does not tarnish. The strip of tinsel is then wound in close turns, well butted up to each other, down to the tail and then wound back up the body to the point it was tied in, cutting off the surplus. This double layer of tinsel means that you avoid the ugly lump at the tail which is unavoidable if you tie it in at the bend. The same thing of course applies with other body materials such as floss silk.

After you have tied in a nice smooth body you reverse the fly in the vice and tie in a hackle of either black hen fibres or scarlet if you want to make the Bloody Butcher version of this fly. The hackle is tied in by the standard 'false or beard' hackling method that I wrote about in the section on the Invicta, in future I shall merely say that a 'false hackle is tied in' and assume that you know what I am talking about!

The fly is now turned right way up again, and we come to the winging; much difficulty is experienced by fly-dressers using the blue feather from a mallard's wing. This is because it is a nasty, intractable feather that once it splits is almost impossible to 'marry' up again, unlike feathers like goose or swan which are very easy to marry. People resort to all sorts of things to avoid using this material, magpie tail feathers, crow or muscovy duck (which, incidentally, I think is the best substitute if you feel you must use something else). All this fuss and bother is not really necessary, however, the blue mallard feather is quite all right as long as you are not afraid of it. As with any other fly-tying material you must handle it firmly; it is a bit like training a dog, it has got to know who is boss! This feather is very prone to splitting and breaking up, and the best way I know of preventing this is to place the slips together ready for winging and then slide them through your mouth to moisten them before they are tied down. In the case of blue mallard this seems not only to make the fibres stick together and to prevent them splitting but it also seems to make the feather more supple.

You will find that many of these feathers are supplied with a heavy curve to the outside edge. Occasionally you find a flattish one, and it is quite surprising how much easier it is to tie in a wing from this type of feather rather than the ones with the pronounced curve. The answer here is moisten a sheet of paper and lay a number of feathers out on top of it, a second sheet is then laid on top of the feathers and a book or a heavy weight is placed on top of the whole 'sandwich'; you will see that after twenty-four hours or so of this treatment you have some very fine, flat and easy to tie winging feathers. This can make things a lot easier, particularly for anyone who has not had a lot of experience.

After the wing is neatly tied in you make a good whip finish and apply a few coats of varnish to the head. Most people only use one coat of varnish but I am a firm believer in having heads as neat, tidy and smooth as it is possible to make them. Aside from anything else it makes them so much more attractive to look at; flies are not just for catching fish, you know, they should be aesthetically pleasing, at least in my book they should!

The Dressing (see Plate 4)

Silk: Black
Tail: Red ibis substitute
Body: Flat silver tinsel or Lurex
Hackle: Black or scarlet hen or soft cock
Wing: Blue mallard wing feather
Hooks: 8 – 14 Old Numbers

JOCK SCOTT

The most effective way of using this rather complicated fly is to fish it really deep on a sunk line. It is a superb fly for picking up better than average fish if used in this way. It does particularly well if you choose to try it on one of those hot, sultry summer days when it seems that nothing is ever going to interest the trout; I always have a couple of these flies in my box for such an occasion. I have never tried this fly on a river but I can imagine no good reason why it should not take fish, its big brother, the fully dressed Jock Scott salmon fly, certainly does. I should imagine that if it was tied on a long-shank low-water iron it would do rather well in the conditions these flies are mainly used for.

Method of tying

This fly is merely a smaller, less complicated version of the salmon pattern, and it is not too difficult to tie once you have got the hang of 'marrying' feather strands to make the wings; that is the only part which might give some problems.

Fix the silk at the eye and wind down to the bend, stop just short of the bend. Now tie in a small tag of scarlet floss silk and on top of this a golden pheasant crest. After these have been tied

Jock Scott (Trout)

in securely, fix in the ribbing tinsel and carry the silk about a third of the way up the hook shank. A piece of golden yellow floss is the next item to go into the dressing and this is run down the shank to the bend and then back up over the first layer to where it was tied in originally. Tie and trim off the surplus. Take the silk up to almost the eye and tie in a piece of black floss, wind this down to butt up to the golden yellow floss and again come back up the body, tie and cut. The body is now ribbed neatly with the tinsel which is also tied in and the end cut off.

The fly is now reversed in the vice and some strands of guinea fowl hackle (not the wing quill fibres) are tied in as a beard. Turn the fly the right way up again in the vice. Now we come to the winging; take your dubbing needle and from both sides of three dyed goose shoulder feathers pick out two strands of each of these colours, yellow, scarlet and blue. This should leave you with six strands of fibre for each half of the wing. Hold the tips of the two left-hand strips of yellow and scarlet in your right hand and stroke towards the tips making certain that the edges are together. You should find that they come together just like a zip fastener – which is all a feather is anyway. After those two colours are joined place the blue strip on top of them and repeat the procedure with that. That will mean that you have half a wing composed of three different colours. When the same thing is done with the other three strips for the other side you have got a married wing which should be just about the right width for a number 10 hook. For larger hooks use extra strands of each colour.

The basic wing is now tied in in the normal wet-fly manner, and after this is done a single strand of peacock sword feather is laid along the top of the wing and tied in at the head. This is usually the most difficult job of all because these feathers tend to spring to one side, but perseverance pays! If you have them, tie in two jungle cock eye feathers each side of the wing; I say 'if you have them' because the import of these feathers is now forbidden by law and anyone who is lucky enough to have any of them left in stock looks on them as gold dust. The best way of fixing these feathers in is to trim off the soft fibres at the base of the hook with scissors so that a jagged edge is left on the stalk. This will then grip the silk and make it far more difficult for the feathers to come adrift. You tie these 'eye' feathers in fairly long and after taking a few turns of silk round the stalk you squeeze the feather gently into the wing with your left hand and pull on the tip of the stalk with your right so that it slides through the turns of silk. This is the only method I know that will ensure that the jungle cock feathers hug tight up to the side of the wing. They should end up quite short with the main 'enamelled' part of the feather almost touching the head of the fly. Finish the head in the normal way and apply two or three coats of a good quality varnish.

The Dressing (see Plate 4)

Silk: Black
Tail: Scarlet floss and a golden pheasant crest
Rib: Oval silver tinsel
Body: Golden yellow and black floss silk
Throat: Speckled guinea fowl hackle
Wing: Married strands of yellow, scarlet and blue goose or
           swan, peacock sword feather over
Sides: Jungle cock
Hooks: 4 – 12 Old Numbers

MARCH BROWN

This is a fly I reserve for fishing downstream and across; the hackled patterns seem to be more killing for upstream work, presumably because the hackles spread all round the body 'work' in the current more. One thing I would say: if you decide to use this fly for this style of fishing, use a limber rod and do not make your leader points too fine, as it is very easy for the leader to get broken on the take with this method of fishing. A fairly heavy leader does not matter too much anyway because the first thing the fish sees is the fly; it is not like trying to present a dry fly upstream cn a heavy leader, which would be hopeless.

I have found that this fly is particularly good in those broken patches of water that most people strive to avoid; the whiter and foamier the water is the better this pattern seems to do. I like to use a fairly short leader, say about six or seven feet and a sink-tip line. This gets the fly down through the first foot or so of water before the swing across current starts; apparently most takes occur as that 'swing' straightens out. It is almost as if the fish followed the fly until it started to slow down a little and then grabbed it. This is the reverse procedure to what normally happens; if a predatory fish is chasing a food item the surest way of making the fish take it is to speed up the movement, as this gives the impression that the food is going to escape. That basic principle does not seem to work with the March Brown, however; it is usually as it slows down that the take comes.

Method of tying

Use a fine brown tying silk and tie in at the eye, carry the silk down the shank to the bend and there tie in two strands of dark brown partridge back feather. If you want to, you can now tie in a piece of olive tying silk for ribbing. This part of the dressing can be omitted if you wish because to my mind it vanishes into the fur body. The only advantage it might give is slight extra strength in that it holds the fur in place if it has been badly dubbed; the answer is to do a good job on the dubbing in the first place.

Dub on the silk a small quantity of hare's fur – I take this from the body of the animal but you can use hare's ear hair if you wish – and wind this up the body to just short of the head. Rib with the tying silk at this point if you used it.

The hook is now turned over in the vice and a hackle of brown partridge is tied in as a beard. Turn the hook the right way up again and tie in a wing composed of two strips taken from a hen pheasant's primary feather (the one you should not use for the Invicta wing if you remember). Finish the head nicely and secure with a good whip finish, varnish the head.

March Brown

The Dressing (see Plate 4)

Silk:	Brown (Sherry Spinner)
Tail:	Two strands of brown partridge back feather
Body:	Hare's fur ribbed with olive tying silk if required
Hackle:	As for tail
Wing:	Hen pheasant primary feather
Hooks:	10 – 14 Old Numbers

DUNKELD

This is one of those patterns I mentioned earlier; a fly that kills fish for everyone but me. The only fish I have ever caught on this fly was a brown trout of about six inches long at Weir Wood, obviously one of the native fish because they never stock with fish of this size. I do wish I knew why I cannot catch fish on this fly, as it is a real favourite with most reservoir anglers I speak to. From the amount of orders I get for it there must be a considerable number of fish caught on it as well; it cannot just be because it is a good-looking fly, pretty to have around, because through the use of jungle cock eye feathers it comes out pretty expensive. No, it really must catch fish, I only wish I knew how, and even more important, why! It certainly does not look like anything I have ever seen swimming in a lake.

Because I have never had a fish worth talking about on this fly it is a little difficult to give you any advice on how or where it should be fished. Some people tell me that it fishes best on the bob, on the point or on a middle dropper – it also seems that it simply must be fished fast, slow or middle-paced at depths varying from right at the bottom in deep water to just sub-surface . . . I think the best thing is for me to leave the fishing of it to you and content myself with telling you how to dress it – that I can do with a reasonable degree of competence!

Method of tying

The style of Dunkeld that seems most popular with my clients is tied in my normal beard hackle style. I have had no complaints about it so presumably it catches fish with reasonable regularity. The original tying had a palmered hackle wound down the hook and ribbed with gold wire or tinsel. I rarely seem to tie this type these days, except perhaps in the larger sizes.

Run the tying silk from the eye to the bend in open spirals. Tie in a golden pheasant crest feather as a tail, wind the tying silk up the shank again, securing the waste end of the crest feather as you go, the second layer of silk forcing the feather's stalk into the first layer to hold the tail really firmly. Catch in a piece of gold tinsel and again take this down the hook to the tail and then back up the body over the first layer to the eye. Do not forget that you will need a little space for tying in the wing and the hackle. Reverse the hook and tie in a false hackle of hot orange. Turn the fly over again and tie in the wing of bronze mallard feather. It can be done perfectly adequately by the 'folded wing method'; this is a very simple way of tying in wings of such materials as bronze mallard or teal. All you do is to take off a strip of feather which is twice the width you want the final wing to be. You straighten this strip out in your fingers as much as possible, so that the tips are level and even, and then you simply fold it in half. This, when it has been licked assumes a neat shape and can be tied in by the usual wet-fly winging method. If you have a bigger fly to dress it can sometimes pay to take two strips from opposing feathers, lay one on the other, fold them in half, and there you have a more dense, tougher wing for such

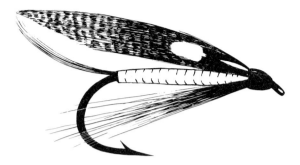

Dunkeld

flies as the strip wing salmon patterns. However, for the Dunkeld just one folded strip is quite sufficient. There are two main advantages to using this method of winging. The first is that flies tied in this way are much faster to dress, and the second is that the colour of the two sides of the wing is always a perfect match. From a professional point of view there is one other great advantage – that is, that there are no waste feathers, the strips can come from feathers taken from either side of the bird and the final wing will look exactly the same, there will be no 'odd' feathers left over.

If you have them the next job is to tie in two small jungle cock eye feathers either side of the wing. These should be tied in quite short so that the shiny part of the feather is close to the head. As always with these feathers they should have the fluffy fibres at the bottom of the stalk removed by clipping with scissors, not by being stripped off; the tiny bits of fibre left on the stalk will then grip the tying silk and the feather will not pull out. Use the same method of tying in that was used in the tying for the Jock Scott.

The Dressing (see plate 4)
Silk: Brown or orange
Tail: Golden pheasant crest
Body: Flat gold tinsel or Lurex
Hackle: Hot orange cock or hen hackle
Wing: Bronze mallard

Sides: Jungle cock 'eyes' or substitute
Hooks: 6 – 12 Old Numbers

PETER ROSS

Of all the standard-pattern trout flies listed in this book the Peter Ross has accounted for more trout for me than any other, that is of course on the reservoirs. I almost invariably fish it on the point if I am using more than one fly. Generally speaking I do not like to use droppers anyway because if there is any wind at all the flies tend to get tangled and consequently if you have not noticed the snarl-up they are not fishing properly. It is pretty time-consuming to be constantly sorting out tangles in the leader, and I find it rather difficult to catch fish unless the fly is in the water!

When I fish this fly I like to use a forward taper sink-tip line. This I combine with a long leader of 12 to 14ft; this means that any line wake is a very considerable distance from the fly. This is important because in my experience this pattern needs to be fished fairly fast and not too deep, so with a short leader on a floating line this 'wake' problem can be considerable. I have proved to my own satisfaction that when fishing this type of fly or any other that requires a shallow, fast retrieve it definitely pays to use as long a leader as conditions will allow.

This is one of the so-called 'attractor' patterns. There are several reasons – or rather theories – about why a trout takes a Peter Ross; one is that it resembles a nymph rising to the surface to hatch (at about three or four miles per hour?). The other, which in my opinion is far more acceptable, is that it looks like a tiny fish; this 'seems' to be the best explanation – that is, until you really think about it. Why will the Peter Ross take fish when far more realistic fry imitations are not even looked at? Why will fish that are taking nymphs or pupae turn aside to take this pattern? I think that the real reason for this is not that it looks like a fish at all, no, it is because it is an annoyance, a competitor, something to be driven from the area of the trout's feeding or, better still, destroyed. I also think exactly the same thing applies to most lures; I am thinking here particularly of the ubiquitous Black Lure. This 'fly' certainly does not resemble anything I have ever seen in the water but the trout take it readily. People say it looks like a leech in the water: all I can suggest is that they take a long, hard look at a real leech sometime. I find it more than a little frustrating not to be able to advance a theory about this apparent anomaly, which is wholly satisfactory, at least to myself. I do think, though, that I am probably nearer the truth than a lot of people with my 'invasion of territory' and 'driving off the intruder' theory. It seems to me that this is the only explanation which really fits all the circumstances.

Method of tying

Put your hook in the vice and give test twangs to it, first downwards, then upwards, to make certain that the temper is correct and that the barb has not been cut too deeply. This knack of testing hooks is quite simple; the tip of your forefinger is placed on the eye of the hook and then taken downwards sharply but smoothly at the same time sliding off the eye; the hook – if it is a good one – should then give a faint 'twang' and if all is well, return to its original shape with no distortion whatsoever. If, however, it is overtempered it will most likely snap off, almost certainly at the bend. If it has been undertempered it will alter its shape and this is where the danger lies. I have seen people who with a soft hook in the vice have straightened it out again and carried on tying the fly! Yes, really I have, they just have not realised that if a hook will do this in a vice it will also do it in a fish – probably the biggest of the season.

Peter Ross

The real bugbear as far as I am concerned is the hook that after a good testing looks fine, but breaks at the barb as soon as a fish is hooked. If you are fishing near rocks or by a reservoir dam wall it is only too likely that the point was broken by being struck on these hard surfaces before the fish ever saw the fly. Far too often, though, the barb has been cut too deeply and at the first pull that tries to 'open up the gape' of the hook it breaks. I well remember the day when I first discovered this major fault: I was out in a boat at Eyebrook reservoir, and I was using a fly with a long-shank size 8 hook. I took six fish on this particular fly with no problems whatsoever then for some reason I got broken on the take. I tied on a new fly of the same pattern. After three or four casts another trout made brief contact, then was gone; a short take, I thought. As always, though, in these circumstances, I checked the hook to make sure it was not blunted or broken. The point was off clean behind the barb. Again I changed the fly and again exactly the same thing happened. And it jolly well kept on happening, six times in all until I ran out of stock of that particular pattern. I was almost gibbering by the time I brought the boat back onto the bank.

Now, when the hook has been tested – and I hope has proved to be a good one – the silk is run down the shank from the eye to the bend in open turns and the tail is fixed in. The ribbing tinsel is tied in at the same point and the silk run up the shank again for about two-thirds of its length. There a strip of flat silver tinsel is tied in and wound down the shank to the tail and then back up again to the place it was first tied in, covering the first layer of tinsel with a second. I prefer to use Lurex where possible on my fly bodies because it does not tarnish, and tarnishing can ruin both the appearance and the effectiveness of any fly.

The next job is to dub on a small amount of either scarlet wool or seal's fur to the silk. You will, if you are a beginner, find the wool easier for this portion of the fly but it does lack some of the sparkle of the stiffer fibres of the fur – not that I think it makes a great deal of difference from the fish's point of view. Run the dubbing up the remainder of the shank, leaving a small space at the eye to receive the hackle and wings. Rib the whole of the body with the tinsel.

Reverse the fly in the vice and tie in a beard hackle of black hen or soft cock's hackle. Remember to trim the hackle to length before it is tied in otherwise it is almost impossible to trim off the odd fibres of hackle once it has been secured to the shank. Turn the fly the right way up again in the vice ready for the winging. Once again for this pattern I find it is better to use the folded-wing method that I described previously. Finish off the head neatly, make a good whip finish and apply a couple of coats of good quality varnish.

The Dressing (see Plate 4)

Silk:	Black
Tail:	Golden pheasant tippet fibres
Rib:	Oval silver tinsel
Body:	Back two-thirds flat silver tinsel or Lurex, front third scarlet wool or seal's fur
Hackle:	Black hen or soft cock
Wing:	Barred teal, widgeon or pintail
Hooks:	8 – 14 Old Numbers

CINNAMON AND GOLD

This fly is one that deserves far greater popularity than it receives at the moment; it is a 'soft' fly, one that is tied in exactly the same way as any other wet fly but the colours give it an ephemeral beauty which is difficult to describe but which is immediately apparent when you look at the fly. The effect is very similar to the Olive and Gold; a blending of the colours into what is obviously a fly which is going to be effective is perhaps the best way of describing it. Anyway, an excellent pattern it certainly is and one that I should hate to be without. The colours are very important, particularly in the wing. A light sepia tone is the shade to aim for, almost an amber.

The Cinnamon and Gold seems to work best for me when it is mounted as a single fly and fished just slightly sub-surface, between, say, a foot and eighteen inches down. The draws of the line are fairly slow and long with very little pause between the pulls. I think I can safely say that every single trout I have taken on this fly was hooked hard in the 'scissors' and when a trout is hooked there it is very rare indeed for it to 'fall off'. People tell me that they take fish on this fly fished as part of a team but I prefer it as a singleton; I have never been very keen on fishing teams of wet flies anyway; there always seems to be some disaster lurking round the corner when I do this, the fish snags me on the loose hook or another fish decides that he fancies the look of the loose fly. Either way it spells problems and the more I can reduce the number of those the happier I feel.

Method of tying

Fix your hook in the vice and test it. Run the silk from the eye to the bend and fix in the tail. This can be of either tippet fibres or, what I prefer, strands of hackle. The silk is taken back up the shank towards the eye, binding down the spare ends of the tail as you do so and the body tinsel is caught in at a point about an eighth of an inch from the eye. This is then wound in close-butted turns down to the tail and then carried back up the shank over the first layer to make a smooth, even body with no lumps or bulges. Tie in and trim off the spare end.

Reverse the fly in the vice and tie in a false hackle of cinnamon or pale ginger hackle fibres. Spread them with your thumb as you tie them in so that the soft outline is maintained. Put the fly the normal way up in the vice and tie in a wing of cinnamon hen wing feathers, keeping the wing fairly slim. After the winging is securely fixed make a neat head and whip-finish; two or three coats of varnish will give a nice glossy look to the head and you

Cinnamon and Gold

will have a fly which a trout should be hard put to resist.

The Dressing (see Plate 4)

Silk: Brown (Sherry Spinner)
Tail: A few strands of cinnamon cock hackle or golden pheasant tippet
Body: Gold tinsel or Lurex
Hackle: As for tail
Wing: Cinnamon hen wing feather
Hooks: 8 – 12 Old Numbers

PARMACHENE BELLE

Over the years I have tried many different fly patterns that originated from America, but I think that this fly has been perhaps the most consistently successful on stillwater fisheries. To the orthodox British eye this fly appears to be extremely gaudy – all of a red and white it is! Do not let it worry you; it is an old-established pattern of proven killing potential. I particularly find this so on those almost hopeless days when the sun blazes down from a clear blue sky. I regard these conditions as a challenge – any reasonable performer with a fly rod can take fish when the conditions are good. It takes bad conditions to sort out the men from the boys. A brace taken under a clear blue sky is worth at least a limit when there is a good breeze and a heavy overcast.

There are at least two totally different methods which can be employed with a fair hope of success on a hot summer's day; you can put on a nymph and inch it along the bottom – certain lures can be used in the same way and often bring good results – but even the most dedicated advocate of the sunk line will admit that it becomes a bit tedious after a while. What I want is a fish or two taken by a method that keeps my interest going. There is a common fallacy among the public (non-angling variety) that the basic requirement for an angler is to have endless patience, to be able to face fishless day after fishless day with stoicism. Just about *every* really successful angler I know becomes very impatient indeed if he is not taking fish, and this very impatience leads him to experiment with different methods until he hits on the one that interests not just himself but the fish as well.

Using a bright fly and fishing it just under the surface can bring really good results. The fascination of watching that vee-wake heading towards the fly can get the adrenalin pumping through the veins of even the most phlegmatic of anglers. Even if the blighter misses it there is still the thought that the very next cast... At least we have moved a fish and, what is more important, seen him move; it puts confidence into our retrieve, in consequence the fly is worked better, and for some strange unfathomable reason the fish is often inspired as well.

It is a fact that two men can fish from a boat and one will take all the fish and the other get nothing. They can be using identical tackle, even switch the tackle from one to the other and still that same man is the one whose fly attracts the interest while the other might as well try fishing in his bath! Surely it can only be because the more successful angler expects to catch fish, he expects a trout to show interest in his fly, therefore the fish does just that. Please do not ask me for an explanation, I am as baffled as the next man. I have sat in boats with men, and sometimes I was the fortunate one and sometimes not (usually the latter!). If I happen to be the one not catching fish, I have done every-thing I can to alter the situation, timed my retrieve to exactly match the other man's length and speed of pull, held my rod at the same angle, cast the same distance, in short done everything I could think of to try to interest a fish – the result? Nothing. Altogether it is a most peculiar business.

Of all the fly patterns that can be classed as 'bright' I don't

Parmachene Belle

think there is one to touch the brilliance of the Parma' Belle. It positively sparkles!

Method of tying

Before setting the hook in the vice it is best to prepare the wings and the tail. Tear off two slim strips from each of the opposing feathers in both colours, red and white duck or goose. Hold the red strip at the bottom and lay the piece of white feather along its upper edge, then stroke the two pieces of web towards the tip, and the two strips will join and become one. Repeat the process with two more strips from the opposing feathers. These make up the tail. Now take a white strip for the bottom part of the wing and marry this to a red strip, then add a further white piece above the red. You should end up with a white wing that has a red stripe running up the centre. Make the other wing half in the same way and lay the tail and wing carefully on one side.

Put the hook in the vice and wind tying silk down the shank in open turns to the bend. Pick up the tail sections and hold the tips together and tie in exactly as you would for an inverted wing so that the natural curves of the strips face inwards and work one against the other. This will ensure that the tail stays perfectly straight. The red should be at the bottom. Make the tail length between half and three-quarters of the body length. Tie in the butt of peacock herl so that the fibres of the flue point towards

PLATE 5: Row I: Mallard and Claret; Greenwell's Glory (wet); Royal Coachman; Alexandra; Row II: Papoose; Cardinal; Harlot; Olive and Gold; Row III: Alder; Teal-winged Butcher; Brown Spider; Black and Peacock Spider

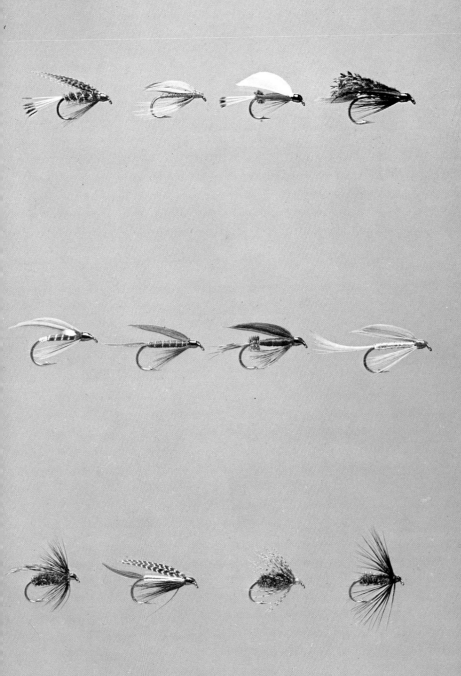

the tail and wind this in close turns from the tail to about a quarter (at most) of the body length. Tie off and cut. Tie in the ribbing tinsel immediately in front of the butt and wind the tying silk up the shank towards the eye of the hook, stopping about an eighth of an inch short of the eye to allow room for the wings and hackle.

Fasten in the floss silk near the eye and wind this down the shank till it is tight up to the butt, then come back over the first layer and tie off at the eye. I usually try to make my floss-silk bodies tapering, slightly carrot-shaped. I think it improves the appearance of the flies, though I am never sure whether the trout appreciate my efforts. If you decide you would like to achieve this effect then take turns of floss back and forth up the body, each layer stopping just short of where the previous layer stopped. This should give a nicely tapering shape. Rib the body neatly with the tinsel and tie in at the eye of the hook.

After you have finished the body reverse the fly in the vice to receive its false hackle. Lay fibres of red hackle stripped from one side of the stalk on the workbench and overlay these with fibres taken from a white hackle. Gather the thick ends of the fibres together, making certain that the tips are level and trim off the thick ends with scissors. Twirl them between your thumb and forefinger and the two colours should mix in together and give a pinkish effect. Trim the hackle to size and tie in at the throat.

PLATE 6: Row I: Eric's Beetle; Black Spider; Lurex Spider; Partridge and Orange; Pennell's Claret; Row II: Black Pennell; Zulu; Sweeney Todd; Church Fry; Row III: Fouracre's Fancy; Whiskey Fly; Oatman's Silver Darter

Reverse the fly in the vice so that it now stands the right way up again.

Take the two prepared wing sections, lay the tips together and tie in in the normal way, finish the head neatly, whip and varnish. In most books on fly-dressing you will read that the wings of this pattern should be of solid white feather with strips of red laid along the sides; you will find that the method I suggest here is far more effective. It gives a much better-looking fly and is really quite simple to do once you get the hang of it.

There is a variation of this pattern called the Parmachene Beau, in which the only real difference is that a rib of oval silver tinsel is used instead of the flat gold and that jungle cock feathers are tied in on each side of the wings. I feel that the real beauty of the Belle is that it is so very bright and gaudy; believe it or not, the jungle cock eye feathers detract from this brightness because this feather, though bright of itself, is dull in comparison to the wings. When I find it necessary to use a really sparkling fly then I do not want anything (even jungle cock) to offset that sparkle. I like my Parmachene Belle completely unadorned!

The Dressing (see Plate 4)

Silk: Black or scarlet
Tail: Red and white duck or goose
Butt: Green peacock herl
Rib: Fine flat gold tinsel or Lurex
Body: Yellow floss silk
Hackle: Red and white cock mixed
Wing: As for tail
Hooks: 6 – 10 Old Numbers

CONNEMARA BLACK

This pattern is one of my personal favourites; it has killed a lot of good trout for me in many different parts of the United Kingdom and in many different types of water.

I well remember fishing an evening rise on a West Country lake. The fish were moving well but could I connect? I tried nearly all my nymphs, various types and shades of midge pupae, all to no avail, not even a swirl. Dry flies were also ignored.

When the light really began to fail and it became impossible to see a fairly large floater at more than about ten feet I decided to try just one last time. I tied on a 'Connie'. A cast of perhaps ten yards over a barely discernable rise form, a draw of the line with my left hand of about a foot, the slack belly at the rod tip straightened and my right hand drew in the hook. The water exploded. The trout – a nice one of about one and a half pounds – fought well, came over the net rim and into the boat.

It was a real pleasure not to have to pack up as soon as darkness fell, for this was a private lake and no restrictions applied – I could have fished all night had I wished to. As it was I fished for about two hours after dark, until about midnight. As soon as complete darkness fell the fish stopped feeding and it was like riding a boat down the river Styx, black, really black. I could no longer distinguish the trees on the bankside against the skyline; the overcast sky and no moon made this as black a night as I have ever fished. After an hour or so and many fruitless casts a tinge of cream painted the horizon, then a silver light fell on the water, and almost immediately the trout began to rise again.

The single fly fell lightly in the path of light from the waxing moon and sat on the surface only semi-submerged. I gave the line a slight tweak and the fly vanished. Almost at once a vee-wake was coming at it from a few feet away so I speeded up the retrieve and suddenly there was a fighting weight on the end of the leader. No leaping rainbow this. He sounded deep into the black depths and the small amount of line I had recovered which lay on the floorboards went whipping through the rings, and I was playing the fish on the reel. After what I imagine must have been ten or twelve minutes we were still virtually even; I had regained line and the fish had promptly taken it back. He was still down deep and the rod-top was curving over in the now bright moonlight. I have often wished I could have had some photographs of that scrap, it was quite spectacular.

Eventually I netted the fish and was astounded that it was not the monster I had expected – later it weighed in at 2lb 7oz, most of that weight on its shoulders – a brownie in the prime of life. My wrist ached for at least three days afterwards. That July night I ended up with five trout, the limit, two rainbows and three brownies, the best fish was just on 3lb, and the smallest was the first one; altogether a lovely couple of hours fishing, and all those trout took the Connemara Black. Since then I have rarely been without it in the box and I look on it as my after-dark fly; it very seldom lets me down.

Method of tying
Set the hook in the vice and after testing it for temper run the tying silk down the shank from the eye to the bend. Secure a crest feather from the golden pheasant as a tail and at the same point tie in your ribbing tinsel. After this wind the silk back up the shank binding down the surplus ends of the feather and tinsel as you go. Just before the eye trim off any excess material and run the silk back down the hook to the tail.

Connemara Black

Black seal's fur is now dubbed onto the silk and a body is wound up the shank and ribbed. In some patterns the hackle is tied in palmer-fashion and secured with the ribbing tinsel but I much prefer a straight false or beard hackle. I have tried both and the beard wins every time. On occasion, though, a hackle of scarlet cock wound palmer-fashion will take fish where the standard dressing will not. After tying in the beard of black cock

116

hackle by reversing the hook in the vice and tying it in underneath it is necessary to add a few fibres of blue jay wing feathers. Turn the fly up the right way again and tie in a slim wing of dark bronze mallard feather. If this fly does not catch fish for you after dark there is very little else that will.

The Dressing (see Plate 4)

Silk: Black
Tail: Golden pheasant crest feather
Rib: Fine oval silver tinsel
Body: Black seal's fur
Hackle: Black cock and blue jay
Wing: Bronze mallard
Hooks: 8 – 14 Old Numbers

MALLARD AND CLARET

This is one of 'those' patterns as far as I am concerned! It is obviously most effective when used on stillwater fisheries; you have only to glance at the record books to establish that fact and see how many fish are taken on the fly to see that it simply must be effective – but not for me.

The Mallard and Claret can be used not just for stillwater trouting but is also excellent (so I am told) for sea trout and general river work. On a lot of the flies I have recommended I have said that wool should be used rather than the normally used seal's fur – for instance the red dubbing on the Peter Ross. On this fly, however, I would only use wool if it was requested by a customer. I feel in this instance you are far better off if you use seal's fur with its flash and sparkle.

Method of tying

Tie in the silk in the normal way from the eye to the bend in open turns and tie in several golden pheasant tippet fibres – I always tie these in so that the lower black band merges into the body. There is no real reason for this except that I reckon it looks neater that way, especially if you are tying up a batch of a gross or so of flies for a client. It is much prettier if all the tails (and the rest of the flies for that matter) look identical. Tie in the tinsel just in front of the tail and run the tying silk up the body and down to the tail again binding down the spare ends of material as you go, trim off any odd bits of tail or tinsel.

Dub the body using seal's fur dyed dark claret – often if you ask a supplier for claret you get a very pale, wishy-washy batch which is nowhere near as good as the darker material – make the body nicely tapered and rib with the tinsel. Reverse the hook and tie in a false hackle. Turn the hook the right way up again and tie in the mallard wing. For most of my mallard (bronze not blue mallard) wings I use the folded-wing method I have described previously, as in the dressing of the Dunkeld for instance.

Mallard and Claret

There is a choice of colours you can use for the hackle on this fly, and all seem to be quite acceptable to the fish. It can be either a dark ginger or pale red hackle or the one which I prefer, a cock hackle dyed to match the body colour, dark claret.

The Dressing (see Plate 5)

Silk:	Claret or brown (Sherry Spinner)
Tail:	Tippet fibres
Rib:	Fine oval gold tinsel or gold wire
Body:	Claret seal's fur
Hackle:	Light red or claret cock
Wing:	Bronze Mallard
Hooks:	8 – 12 Old Numbers

GREENWELL'S GLORY

This is the wet version of the fly in Chapter One, and I believe that the late Canon used the wet version rather than the dry. Dry-fly fishing at that date was in its infancy and certainly was not in general use in Scotland at that time – it is not very popular in that country to this day, most anglers seeming to prefer the sunk patterns.

Reservoir anglers take a lot of fish on the wet Greenwell. It is generally assumed that the 'humpy-backed' effect the wing gives is reminiscent of a nymph. This may be the case but certainly there are much more precise copies of nymphs which do not catch fish. I am inclined to think that if a fly is put in front of a feeding trout and it is roughly the right size and coloration then the odds are the fish will try it and see what its food value is; in this case it is nil. I have used this fly to good effect on many reservoirs and even if the retrieve is fairly fast it still catches fish, which would seem to suggest that the trout do not take it for a nymph but rather a small fry, a baby perch perhaps?

Method of tying

This is one of the few flies where I wax my silk (nasty, messy stuff!) and it is necessary to get the correct body colour which should be a dirty, yellowy olive shade that is best arrived at by using a pale primrose silk and liberally smarming it up with wax! I have tried using different shades of olive silk but it still does not seem quite right. So I am afraid that wax it has to be.

Start the tying silk at the eye and carry it down the shank in close, touching turns until just before the bend starts, at this point catch in your ribbing wire and make the 'spare end' go up the shank almost to the eye. This is because you will get a really good fixing if the rib is bound in all the way up the body and also if it is snipped off short you are left with a hump which could easily be avoided, I do like the body on this fly to be nice and even. Carry the silk back up the shank to the eye, again the turns of silk should be even and touching. Rib the body with the wire, make the turns nicely even, as nothing spoils a fly more than uneven ribbing. The turns of the rib should be fairly close together, about three wire diameters apart should be just about right.

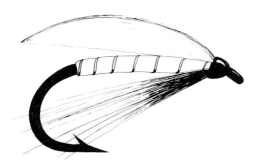

Greenwell's Glory (wet)

The fly should now be turned over in the vice to receive its beard hackle; this is of furnace cock and is rather scarce, a good one at any rate. I have found a way round this; there has been a lot of talk in recent years of using the marker felt-tip pens for marking up hackles and they certainly work very well but normally the marking is done on a sheet of paper with the whole feather laid flat out. It is perfectly simple to mark up hackles by tearing off a bunch, trimming the butts to length and then rubbing them (again on paper) with a black marker pen. If an ordinary ginger or light red hackle is chosen then you get the precise effect of the furnace hackle at a tenth the cost of the real thing. The ink is waterproof so there is very little danger of its washing off, and the results are excellent. I much prefer using the big hackle at the base of the cape for false hackles. Precisely the same method can be used to produce, say, Badger hackles for tying in as a beard. These pens are extremely useful and I always have a selection of different colours by me so that if a hackle, or the hackle stalk etc, needed for a particular pattern is not available I can dye one up on the spot. For such flies as the Lunn patterns they are the ideal answer, certainly so if you only require small quantities of a given colour or shade.

The hackle is tied in and the fly is now turned up the right way to accept the wing. This is nowadays generally the web taken from a starling's primary feather. Originally it was that of a blackbird but nowadays these birds are protected – and a jolly good thing too, I think of all the British songbirds the sound of a blackbird in full song is the finest. The only reason people rave about nightingales is because they sing at night, and consequently they have no competition; I should hate not to be able to listen to the blackbird. There is a way of getting blackbird wing feathers, though, if you absolutely insist on them. Many of these birds are killed by traffic on our roads and you can always do a swift amputation of the wings of one of these casualties. It is all a bit ghoulish, though, and generally speaking I prefer to stick to the starling wing feather, there are always plenty of those around!

Tie in the two strips of web by the usual method and finish the head neatly, make a good whip and apply two or three coats of varnish. I cannot stress this too strongly, half-hitches are no substitute for a whip finish. I know fly-dressers who never apply any varnish at all to the heads of their flies but they still do not fall apart, and why? Simply because they are using a whip finish with four or five turns of silk holding everything firm. If you tried fishing with a fly finished off with half hitches and no varnish I doubt very much indeed if it would last much beyond the second cast. The thing to remember is this; after most varnishes have been immersed in water for any length of time they soak off, the varnish lifts, it cracks or it peels off, as they are not a permanent finish – not by any means. So use a whip and be safe, it is really quite easy to learn, honestly! If you really cannot master it with your fingers then you can always use one of those whip-finish tools that are on the market these days, though I myself regard them as cheating.

The Dressing (see Plate 5)

Silk:	Primrose
Body:	Primrose tying silk, well waxed
Rib:	Gold wire
Hackle:	Furnace cock
Wing:	Starling primary feather
Hooks:	12 – 14 Old Numbers

ROYAL COACHMAN

The Royal Coachman was invented in Great Britain but it gained its real popularity in America, and so I always think of it as a 'furriner', though really it is only an expatriate.

The dry Coachman – especially dressed with hacklepoint wings, as I said in the first chapter – is one of my firm favourites, but the wet version has never really achieved the results that I had hoped for. But the Royal Coachman with its flash of scarlet body really does 'bring home the bacon' for me.

There was an extraordinary day at Weirwood reservoir in Sussex, for instance. The water surface on that mid-June day was that hopeless dull brass colour and had been like that all the morning. I had stopped fishing because there seemed no point in continuing with conditions as they were. I was eating my sandwiches and admiring the lush summer surroundings when I spotted a bird of some kind high over the dam – I was half-way up the reservoir at the time, in a boat. I thought at first it was a heron, it was pretty big even at that distance . . . Then, as it crossed the dam it closed its wings and fell like a stone, I could just make out the splash as it hit the surface. It rose from the water and flew directly towards me. As it came closer I realised that what I was looking at was an osprey, that rare fish-hawk that is just beginning to re-establish itself in Scotland as one of our native breeding species. It was a magnificent sight; it came directly over my head and as usual when I really needed it, I did not have a camera. It had caught a trout that appeared to be about a pound and a half, a much more efficient fisherman than I was! I watched it move out of sight behind some pine-trees on the North bank.

When I later spoke to Ken Sinfoil, the head bailiff, he said that these beautiful birds often visited the reservoir; so you never know, we might eventually have a breeding colony establish itself in 'wildest Sussex'. I have never seen one since but I live in hopes and now when I go there to fish I always, but always, carry a camera.

The day had not finished with me yet though, I was to be given another glimpse of an extraordinary feature of this lovely lake, its very big and so far largely uncaught brown trout. I saw some fish moving about sixty yards away over the deeper water. Very gently I eased the oars into the rowlocks and pulled gently in the direction of the boils. About twenty yards away I silently shipped the oars and let the boat carry on with its gentle glide through the water. There were about a dozen of them, and what trout they were. I had plenty of time to study them at extremely close quarters and I do not believe that one of them was under four pounds and several must have approached the 6 or 7lb mark. All brownies, and they appeared to be in lovely condition.

I cast nearly every fly pattern in the box at those fish and they totally ignored the lot. They were not feeding; they were playing just like otters, sliding and gliding, round, over and under one another, breaking surface in a flurry of spray and then diving deep, the performance repeated time and again. I fished for and watched those trout for at least half-an-hour, then, as if a switch had been thrown they went down and that was the last I saw of them.

Half-way back to the fishing lodge, or the boathouse as it then was, I again saw fish rising. I cast, and there was an immediate pull. The hook was set and I netted a brownie of 12oz. In an hour I took a limit bag of eight fish – all on the Royal Coachman. There were no really large fish in the bag; according to my fishing diary the best weighed 15oz. But what a splendid end to a most unusual and interesting day, I was very pleased with both myself and Weirwood reservoir!

The Royal Coachman is not just a fly to catch fish with; it is also a marvellous friend-impresser. It looks good with its bright, sharp contrasts of colours and materials. It is also fairly easy to tie. If you have experienced any difficulty with winging wet flies then duck primary quills are the feathers for you.

Method of tying
Start the silk slightly back from the eye and carry it down to the bend where you catch in a few strands of golden pheasant tippet and a piece of peacock herl. The peacock needs to have a long bronze coloured flue; these are normally found about half-way down the 'eye' feather from a peacock's tail. Tie in the tip of the strand so that the flue points back over the tail and wind several turns close together so that you have neatly shaped 'butt'. Wind the tying silk over the spare end of the peacock herl and leave it sticking beyond the eye of the hook – you will need it again in a minute.

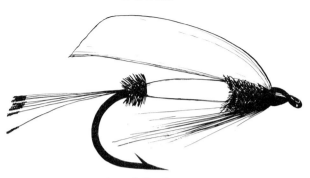

Royal Coachman

About two-thirds of the way up the body (where you should have left the silk hanging after you wound it over the herl) you catch in a strand of scarlet floss silk. If you buy the two-strand twisted type of floss then you will need to separate the strands, otherwise you can go mad trying to get smooth bodies! I have found the best way is to separate one strand from the other and cut a piece off just one of the sides; by this method you can work your way through the spool without having to separate the strands each time you need to use that particular colour. It is much more satisfactory than just cutting off the twisted floss and separating it once it is cut. Wind the floss silk back and forth over the shank until you build up a nice, smooth, carrot-shaped body, tie in where you started winding and cut off the surplus. Now take the loose end of the peacock herl (it is sticking out to the front, or at least it should be!) and wind another butt just in front of the body.

Reverse the fly in the vice and tie in a false hackle of either ginger or light red cock hackle fibres. Turn the fly the right way up again and tie in a wing of white duck primary feather. This is one of the few exceptions I make to my normally very slim wings, the wider strips of web seem to do better for me on this pattern.

The Dressing (see Plate 5)

Silk: Brown (Sherry Spinner) or black
Tail: Golden pheasant tippet
Body: Back quarter and forward quarter, bronze peacock herl; centre, scarlet floss silk

Hackle: Ginger cock
Wing: White duck primary feather
Hooks: 8 – 14 Old Numbers

ALEXANDRA

This is a fly that at one time was considered to be so deadly that it was banned on some waters. While I have never found it to be quite so effective it does sometimes take fish where little else will, and that is the reason for its inclusion in this book. It is not the be-all-and-end-all of flies by any means, no fly is, thank the Lord, or it would put us professional fly-dressers out of business! It is just another pattern that is always worth having along.

When I have used it – mainly on the reservoirs – it seems that it catches far more fish if the retrieve is fairly fast. I have done best when using a forward taper, sink-tip line when the fly has been allowed to sink to about three or four feet before the retrieve is started.

Method of tying
For the first three operations, tail, body and hackle, it is exactly the same as the procedure used to tie the Silver Butcher so there is no point in repeating it here; only the winging is different.

After the hackling has been completed the fly is turned upright in the vice and a wing of peacock sword feather is tied in. This

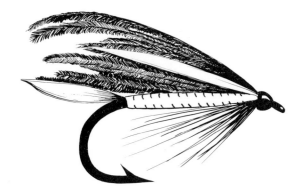

Alexandra

is possibly the most difficult wing of all for the newcomer to fly-dressing. The separate fibres tend to spring out in all directions and the fly ends up looking like a green, red and silver hedgehog! The secret is not to tear the fibres off the stalk but to cut them off with a very sharp knife, and cut a piece out of the quill with them, this way they do not tend to spring in all directions anywhere near as easily. Whatever you do do not lick this feather; it might make it easier to tie in but it ruins its appearance. Of course, whether the fish care in the slightest is quite another matter, I am thinking of it from the aesthetic point of view.

When after much struggling you have got the wing tied in as neatly as you can, you will be happy to hear that the next operation can be even trickier! What you have to do is to tie in a strip of scarlet goose or duck feather either side of that wing; if you are not extremely careful you will find that these strips will also tend to stick out to the side. There is, however, a trick of the trade, that Collyer will now reveal. Tie in the strip of feather so that it is a shade too long, an eighth of an inch is enough, take two or three turns of silk over it and then grip the butt-end tightly and slide it through the silk until it is the correct length. Do not ask me to explain why it works in keeping the strip close to the wing, I do not know, but work it does if it is done correctly. You use exactly the same principle for tying in jungle cock feathers– if you happen to be lucky enough, or wealthy enough to have any! Tie in the two strips using the procedure described above and then finish off the head, whip and varnish. If you have got some jungle cock feathers and you tie these in instead of the strips of scarlet your fly becomes what is known as the Jungle Alexandra; I myself prefer the scarlet strips.

The Dressing (see Plate 5)

Silk: Black
Tail: Ibis substitute
Body: Silver tinsel or flat Lurex
Hackle: Black cock
Wing: Peacock sword feather with scarlet strips down each side, duck or goose
Hooks: 8 – 10 Old Numbers

PAPOOSE

One of my favourite streamer flies is the Chief Needabeh, and the Papoose is his offspring. Sometimes it is necessary to use a fly smaller than the normal streamer sizes while at the same time retaining the same colour and flash – if not quite as much action. I have had days when the fish tweaked and pulled the wings of the streamer but missed the part that mattered, the hook point, every time. The Papoose was invented for those occasions. I do not like scaling down the streamer flies too much, size 10 is all right but I do not like going much under that, and this wet-fly pattern has served me very well as a substitute.

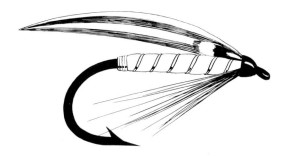

Papoose

It is exactly the same dressing as the Chief Needabeh except for the wings which are of eight married strips of goose feather (like a built-wing salmon fly) and the hackle, which is tied in as a beard, not wound as it is in the bigger version. The fly should be used in exactly the same way as the streamer and at the same sort of time; bright, sunny days and stripped in fast just under the surface. Those old trout fair tear after it!

Method of tying

Run black tying silk from the eye to the bend in open turns, stopping just short of the bend in fact and then winding close-butted turns of silk for about an eighth of an inch (on the bigger hook sizes). Close turns at the bend are needed otherwise the tag will not sit neatly. Tie in a piece of oval silver tinsel, and wind a neat tag of about three or four turns, going from the back of the close turns of silk forward towards the eye, tie in but do not trim off the surplus.

Run the tying silk back up the shank towards the eye and catch in a piece of scarlet floss silk. Wind a carrot-shaped body so that it meets the tag neatly without any overlapping, finish winding the silk at the eye end of the hook, tie and trim. Rib the body evenly with the tinsel and fix this and trim off at the same point.

Turn the fly over in the vice to receive the beard hackle; for mixing the two colours of hackle together use the same procedure as described for the Parmachene Belle; scarlet and yellow this time, though, not scarlet and white. The same process of making up the wings is used as in the Parma' Belle as well, except that four strips each side are used instead of three, and the colours go in this order, from the bottom: orange, yellow, orange and again yellow. If you have any jungle cock feathers then tie them in on either side of the wings so that just the first 'enamelled' patch is showing, no more than that or you will hide the wings, and after all your hard work at marrying them you would not want that, would you?

The Dressing (see Plate 5)

Silk:	Black
Tag:	Oval silver tinsel
Rib:	As for tag

PLATE 7: Row I: Spencer Bay Special; Chief Needabeh; Grey and Red Matuka; Ace of Spades; Row II: Red Queen; Black and Silver Matuka; Matuka Badger Lure; Black Lure; Row III: White Lure; Sinfoil's Fry; Grafham Polystickle; Muddler Minnow

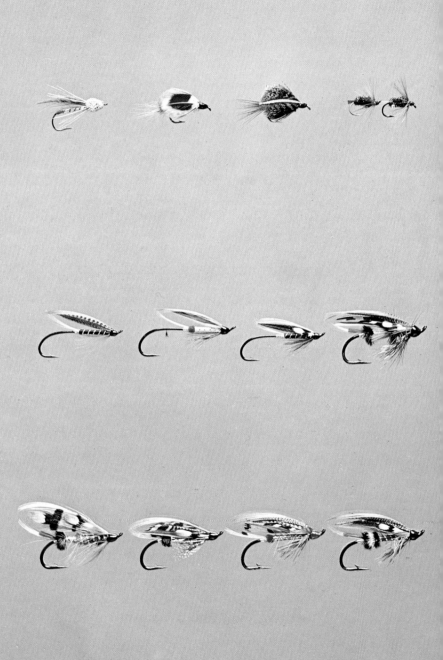

Body: Scarlet floss silk
Hackle: Mixed scarlet and yellow cock, as a beard
Wings: Married strips of orange, yellow, orange and yellow swan or goose
Sides: Jungle cock eye feathers
Hooks: 8 – 12 Old Numbers

CARDINAL

There are occasions when the trout will only look at a fly which is tied of material of only one colour, and it has been my experience that when this happens that colour is either orange or red. One cannot be dogmatic about it, of course, and I can only tell you what has been happening to me. I once fished a bay at Weir Wood reservoir and I kept getting short takes to a Royal Coachman (which has a scarlet main body, of course). These takes were coming at fairly frequent intervals but I just could not get a solid take for the life of me. The angler in these circumstances is left with two choices; he can either persist with the pattern of fly that he is using in the hope – usually forlorn – that the fish will grow more ambitious and take firmly, or he can do what I did on this particular occasion, switch flies until he comes up with something that really does appeal to the trout. I went right through the box and eventually it dawned on me – I am a bit slow on the uptake sometimes! – that the only flies that were interesting the fish at all were the patterns with red in them.

PLATE 8:   Row I: Whiskey Muddler; Leslie's Lure; Walker's Killer; Wormfly; Row II: Blue Charm; White Doctor; Thunder and Lightning; Jock Scott (salmon); Row III: Durham Ranger; Mar Lodge; Blue Doctor; Collyer's Blue

Colour photographs by Alistair Dumbell.

I promptly skipped the remainder of the flies in the box and tied on the solitary size 10 Cardinal that nestled in a corner. Out of six casts I took five fish, each one hooked solidly in the scissors. I must have been getting a bit wrought up by this time because I did not bother to check the leader and the next fish broke off and took my single Cardinal with him. When I looked at the leader I saw why he had broken me: the bottom half-inch or so was very badly frayed indeed, trout have extremely sharp teeth! I fished on for the remainder of that day without landing any fish. I had 'short takes' to any fly that contained an element of red in its dressing but that was all. If I had had my portable fly-dressing kit with me that day I am perfectly certain that I should have had a limit bag in no time at all. Nowadays, of course, I am rarely if ever without it, and many is the time it has saved the day for me.

Method of tying

Run the tying silk from the eye to the bend of the hook in open turns and tie in a tail of two strips of a scarlet dyed duck feather (Ibis substitute) as I have already described for the Butcher. At the same point fix in a piece of fine gold wire. Wind the tying silk back up the shank of the hook binding down the end of the tail feather and the wire as you go, catch in a piece of scarlet floss silk and wind this down the hook to the tail and then back up the body over the first layer and tie off and trim at the eye end. Rib evenly with the wire.

Turn the fly over in the vice to receive the false hackle which

Cardinal

is of scarlet cock hackle, turn the fly the right way up again and tie in the wings which are of the same material as the tail. Do a good whip finish of at least four turns of silk and apply two or three coats of a good-quality clear varnish to the head.

The Dressing (see Plate 5)

Silk: Scarlet or black
Tail: Ibis substitute
Rib: Fine gold wire
Body: Scarlet floss silk
Hackle: Scarlet dyed cock hackle
Wing: As for tail
Hooks: 8 – 12 down eye, Old Numbers

HARLOT

This is one of those patterns that surprise you! It was not tied for any really good reason initially, I was just sitting at my fly-tying bench with a few minutes to spare, started fiddling with materials, and this was the pattern that emerged; I did not for one minute think that it could possibly turn out to be a good fish-taker but surprisingly it has. During the early part of the 1972 season I used it sometimes on the reservoirs just to see if it would get any response. It caught fish – not a fantastic number, or for that matter very large fish, but it did take several quite reasonable trout. The few I have tied up and dispatched to clients have also caught fish so for that reason alone I think it might be worth sparing it a little space in this book. If nothing else it is a good exercise in

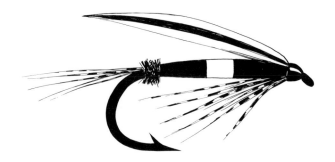

Harlot

fly-dressing and even if you never use it the Harlot will certainly liven up a dark corner of your fly-box!

Method of tying

For this fly, the Harlot – I like that name, it must be my warped sense of humour – carry the silk from the eye to the bend of the hook and catch in a few fibres of dyed blue gallena (guinea fowl) hackle as a tail. Then wind a butt of bronze peacock herl, not too long. Now catch in a strand of black floss silk and wind a carrot-shaped rear section for the body; tie down and wind a centre section of scarlet floss, then finish the front of the body with black floss again.

Reverse the hook in the vice, tie in a false hackle of blue gallena. Marry up strands of scarlet and black dyed goose feather as you did for the Parmachene Belle with the scarlet to the outside of the winging strip and a black centre stripe. Hold the tips of the two strips together so that they match perfectly then tie them in in the normal wet-fly style; whip-finish and varnish the head. If this fly does not remind you of a 'woman of easy virtue' then my name is not Collyer!

The Dressing (see Plate 5)

Silk: Black
Tail: Blue gallena
Butt: Bronze peacock herl
Body: In three sections, black, scarlet and black floss silk
Hackle: Tied as beard, blue gallena
Wing: Married strands of scarlet, black and scarlet goose
Hooks: 6 – 8 down eye, Old Numbers

OLIVE AND GOLD

There can be little excuse for inventing wet flies with standard-type dressings because there are so many already available, ninety per cent of which are, at best, only mediocre fish-takers, and some are downright useless. It is therefore with some trepidation that I offer you this fly for examination. I have taken quite a few fish on it, and the Olive and Gold – as I said in the passage about the Cinnamon and Gold – is a 'soft' fly, not really bright at all, even though you might think so from the colours involved.

I cannot say why it is that certain flies look like good fish-killing patterns to me and others do not, but one thing is certain: the moment I tied this pattern I knew that trout would want it, and I was very happy when they proved me right! With its bright gold body and gold tail it blends in with the mixed feather wing in such a way that it has that certain 'feel' to it; I simply knew that the trout would want to try it for taste.

Method of tying

Wind the tying silk from the eye to the bend and tie in a fairly long golden pheasant crest as a tail. Wind the silk back up the shank binding down the waste-end of the crest feather as you go. Just behind the eye tie in a strip of flat gold tinsel or Lurex and wind down the shank in even, close-butted turns until you reach the point where the tail was tied in, then, as is usual in my style of dressing, come up over the first layer to the eye and tie off. If you find at any time that a trout's teeth are cutting the tinsel bodies, not just on this fly but on any of the patterns I have mentioned, it can pay to rib the tinsel with fine wire of the appropriate colour. This will help to protect the bodies and if they do become cut they will not unravel to anywhere near the same degree. Lurex in particular is liable to this fault because it is so soft, its virtue of being immune to tarnishing, however, outweighs any of its faults in my opinion.

Reverse the fly in the vice and tie in a hackle of ginger cock

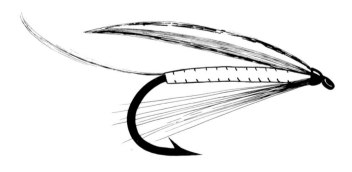

Olive and Gold

as a beard, do not forget to try and 'spread' the fibres round the hook shank as you tie in.

Take the fly out of the vice and turn it the right way up again; we are now coming to the winging. Once again this is a 'married' wing of different-coloured strips of goose feather and these, as the name implies, are of olive and gold. Join the strips together in the same manner as that used during the tying of the Parmachene Belle and the Harlot. The olive-dyed goose strips are the outside sections and the gold is the inside stripe; tie in the wing and finish the head in the usual way.

The Dressing (see Plate 5)

Silk:	Brown (Sherry Spinner)
Tail:	Golden pheasant crest
Body:	Flat gold tinsel or Lurex, ribbed gold wire if necessary
Hackle:	Ginger cock
Wing:	Married strands of goose, olive, gold and olive
Hooks:	6 – 8 Old Numbers

ALDER

It is not very often that I fish a river by the 'down-stream and across' method; not because I think it is not a successful method, far from it. The reason is that there is to my mind very little skill needed to take fish in this way; certainly this is true of trout. You cast your fly – or flies – nearly straight across the river, make perhaps one or two upstream mends in the line to slow down their travel and just wait until a fish grabs hold of the feathered offering. Not a very demanding method.

I make one exception to this general opinion, however, and that is with the Alder when I am fishing for grayling. I am not, of course, including salmon fishing where this is the standard technique, and very nearly the only possible one. Where I find that grayling are holed up in a position that is nearly impregnable from a downstream position, and I cannot use either a dry fly or a nymph to catch them, then I start in on the downstream and across. The fly that is almost invariably the most useful for this is the Alder. The grayling seem to find it irresistible in most circumstances, and, oddly, it does not have to be in season. There need not have been a natural on the water for months, they still have a go at the artificial.

There are two major snags when using this technique; one is that often fish come adrift because they are lightly hooked in the front of the mouth, and the strike tends to pull the hook out of their mouths rather than drive it into the scissors as it would if the angler were downstream of the fish. The other major problem is that of leader strength; if a big fish decides to take the fly then there is every possibility of a break on the strike, particularly if the rod is pointed downstream. The rod must be kept at an angle to the current so that the top can absorb the shock of the take. The leader strength should be at least double that used for upstream work. If you have been taking fish of say a pound on a point tapering to two pounds' breaking strain then I would say a minimum of four pounds for fishing downstream with perhaps another pound or two added as a safety margin.

I have already said that I consider the Alder primarily as a grayling pattern. Some people, I have no doubt, will find they do well with trout on this fly – not I, I do not think that one single trout has ever taken this fly, and I have tried it often enough both on rivers and stillwaters; but then, that has only been my personal experience and, as we all know, a fly which takes any number of fish for one man will not take a single trout for someone else.

Method of tying
Run black tying silk down the hook shank from just behind the eye to just in front of the bend, do not 'go round the corner'. Open turns of silk are fine tie in several strands of peacock herl, twirl them together to make a 'rope' just as you did for the Hacklepoint Coachman and wind them up the shank over wet varnish. Tie in and trim off the ends about a quarter of the way down the shank from the eye; this is to allow room for the wings and hackle.

Tie in a wing of two strips taken from opposing feathers of brown speckled hen's wing. When the wings are firmly set on the hook tie in a fairly long-fibred dyed black hen's hackle and, starting from the eye end, wind it back in close, touching turns

Alder

to meet the wing. Tie in the tip of the feather and trim off the spare end, wind the silk carefully through the hackle keeping it taut at all times to avoid squashing the fibres out of position, and with your left hand hold the hackle back so that it lies slightly back. Two or three turns of silk should hold it in position – the fibres should be just a shade out of the vertical so that the fly will be less inclined to behave as a dry fly. It never fails to amaze me just how splendid wet flies are at floating and dry flies at sinking! Make a neat whip finish and apply a couple of coats of varnish to the head.

The Dressing (see Plate 5)

Silk: Black
Body: Peacock herl
Wings: Speckled hen's wing
Hackle: Dyed black hen
Hooks: 10 – 14, down eye, Old Numbers

TEAL-WINGED BUTCHER

I seem to have an irresistable urge to mess about with fly patterns in the hope of making some tiny improvement on the original. I am still not sure why I tied this fly up in the first place, but it certainly looked good both in the vice and in the water. It hit the jackpot for me about three years ago at Chew Valley Lake – those brownies went wild for it. It proved useful not just on the Bristol lakes but as a good standby general pattern.

From the tying point of view it is certainly **easier** to make a decent wing by using teal breast feather as opposed to the normal blue mallard wing feathers; of course this only really applies to beginners in fly-dressing. Once a tyer has had a little experience it does not matter what feathers he is using, they should all be equally easy. I well remember, though, the trouble I had with blue mallard when I first started; I tried various alternatives in an attempt to find a more tractable feather. Magpie tail and muscovy duck back feathers were two that worked fairly well, I remember, but they did not have that lovely rich blue sheen of the mallard feather.

On that particular trip to Chew I had been talking to several anglers who had been down for a fortnight or more, and the only flies that had been taking fish were the big lures, mainly Black lures tied with three hooks. One chap had had a fish or two on a Wormfly, but it was all rather discouraging for somebody who is not too keen on multi-hook rigs in the first place. I decided that the only thing to do was to explore and experiment, and for this approach to reservoir trouting there is no substitute for a boat, it would certainly be worth staking four pounds just for mobility's sake. It is a lovely feeling when all you have got to do is to start the motor and go straight across the lake to another spot without having to worry about carting all the gear back to the car and driving round by road; I mostly fish from the banks but where possible I like a boat purely as a means of transport. The main idea was that I should have a good look round, find where the fish were feeding and then for the remaining afternoon and full day of the trip hammer 'em from the bank at the lower price!

Like all my best-laid plans it went right up the proverbial creek! I toured round like a good 'un; nothing on the dam, nor as far as I could see on any of the headlands, bank or bays. The lake looked as dead as that lake ever can be. Then I decided to take my lunch on Denny Island, and of course that is where the blighters were, gobbling away at the roach fry with big bow waves sweeping in from the deep water and the small fish scatter-ing in panic along the surface. So much for my 'cheap' trip . . . I had to have a boat to get at them – I was pleased I was not down for a week. My bank manager would have died of shock!

I tried many different flies to take those fish and the only trout that came my way was a brownie of about two and a half pounds that picked up a Polystickle 'on the drop'. Many times I have found that the best way by far to take these fry-chasing trout is not to employ any retrieve at all in the first stages of the cast, merely to cast in the general direction of the turmoil and just let the fly sink under its own weight. This is because the trout likes to sweep into the attack on a whole shoal of little 'uns, but that attack is not based on the idea of capturing a fish, it is designed to injure, stun and generally disable as many as possible. Old Mister Trout then comes back quietly and mops up the casualties at his leisure. Of course I cannot be absolutely certain of this theory but observation over a considerable number of years sug-gests that this is so.

It is the powerful swing-round at the end of the charge with the tail and the body turning and beating the water (and the fry) that does the damage. There must be an awful lot of turbulence and disturbance created in those close-packed ranks of tiny fish, the shock waves must be fearsome. This theory also accounts for the long pauses between the raids that are so common a feature of the 'sticklebacker'. It also seems quite likely to me that the trout hunt in packs on these occasions with one fish hitting the shoaling fry and the others then coming in after him and cleaning up. Perhaps this is why it is quite possible to take several fish, one after the other, in a spot where you would swear there was only one trout having a go at them.

The upshot of the matter was that although I had had that one fish on the 'Poly' no more fish were particularly keen so I went on trying different patterns of fly until I eventually came to the untried Teal-winged Butcher, and from the moment I tied it on I started taking fish steadily. I had a marvellous three days – up to my eyes in trout I was! Great stuff! A peculiar thing, though; they were all brownies, not a rainbow amongst them.

Method of tying

Start the silk just behind the eye and carry it down the shank to the bend of the hook in open turns (gaps between the turns of silk), at the bend tie in your two strips of ibis substitute just as you did for the Silver Butcher. The silk is now wound back up the body over the waste ends of the tail feather, binding it down tight into the under-layers of silk; as I have said previously, a tail tied in by this method will never come adrift. You then trim off the spare ends of the feather just behind the eye, catch in a piece of flat silver tinsel or Lurex and wind this down the shank in even, close-butted turns to meet the tail and then come back up the body over the first layer to the eye, tie in and trim off the surplus. Reverse the fly in the vice and tie in a throat hackle of black hen hackle, then turn the fly the right way up in the vice again. Take a wide strip of prime-quality teal breast feather, straighten it in your fingers and then gently fold it exactly in half, tie in your wing and cut off the spare end of the winging feather with scissors. Make a neat head, whip-finish and apply two or three coats of varnish.

The Dressing (see Plate 5)

Silk:	Black
Tail:	Ibis substitute
Body:	Flat silver tinsel or Lurex
Hackle:	Dyed black hen tied as beard
Wing:	Barred teal breast feather
Hooks:	8 – 12 Old Numbers

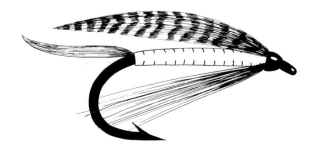

Teal-winged Butcher

CHAPTER NINE

HACKLED WET FLIES

BROWN SPIDER

They say that the Black and Peacock Spider imitates a snail; well, I do not believe it. Dick Walker's *Pelletus vulgaris* looks far more like a snail, even if your ethics might be called into question if you used it! The B. and P. (a Tom Ivens invention) has taken a lot of fish for a lot of people, and just what the trout take it for I have no idea, but I will bet it is not a snail. The normal retrieve of this pattern is the figure-of-eight gather and even at its slowest that old 'snail' is doing a real gallop! Have you ever watched a freshwater snail move? It is going at a fair pace if it covers an inch in five minutes.

When the reservoir angler thinks of spider patterns it is almost invariably the B. and P. that comes to his mind, but there are others that are equally good at taking fish. One of the best is the Brown Spider, and it will take trout where the other fly will not. Now I come to think of it, perhaps that name 'spider' is the real clue; maybe that really is *just* what the trout take it for. There are species of spider that live underwater. They build nests of air bubbles and are constantly going backwards and forwards to the surface to replenish the supply. I have spent many an hour, completely fascinated, watching them. Perhaps this is why the spider patterns are at their best when used close up to weed-beds – the nests are always secured to the underside of a water plant. Anyway, they certainly move a lot faster than any snail, and it seems a reasonable theory to me.

It is a peculiar thing that the Brown Spider is not effective as a fish-taker on all stillwaters. For instance, it works on the Bristol reservoirs but not at Weir Wood; it did not do too well for me at Grafham either. I did not get the chance for a really good testing there so I cannot be absolutely certain, but I do know from a client that the fish at Eyebrook (just up the road a few miles from Grafham) have been going mad for it. I suppose it is just a case where you will have to tie up a few and try them on your local water and see just what results you get; if the fish really do want them the resulting sport can be quite spectacular.

The best way to fish it that I have found is to grease the leader to within about four or five feet of the fly, find some weed-beds in shallowish water (not much more than five feet deep) and try and fish it parallel to those weeds, along the edge of the bed. A boat is perhaps the best way of doing this, provided that you have an anchor at either end so that you can fish the fly slowly and in the precise location of the edge of that weed-bed. All you do then is 'cast 'er out, let 'er sink and then pull 'er back in again'; slow pulls of a foot or so at a time seem best. Try *not* to make any more of a pause between the pulls than you have to, because the natural does not sink back on its way to the surface. You can be prepared for takes either when the fly is sinking or on the retrieve and those takes can be extremely vicious so do not use too weak a leader – unless of course you actually *like* losing fish.

Method of tying

All the spider patterns are very easy to tie. In fact if I am teaching somebody to tie flies I always start them off with the spiders. I think it is encouraging when the very first fly a beginner ties looks as if it would catch fish – as indeed it probably will. It also helps when the instructor can look at that fly and with sincerity say, 'Oh yes, a fly that the trout would definitely want.' So much better than lying through your teeth, don't you think?

Use a brown tying silk and wind down the shank to the bend – not round it – and catch in a bunch of peacock herl strands – four or five should be all right. If you are going to wind the body in a clockwise direction, then twirl the strands together anti-clockwise so that they form a rope effect, then wind them up the body to just behind the eye. Secure with the tying silk and trim off the surplus.

Wind on a hackle of brown partridge back feather. I usually tear off the bottom fluffy fibres then gently tease down the remainder except for a few at the very tip of the hackle, which I tie in.

Brown Spider

I then clip the hackle pliers to the stalk of the hackle and wind it from there (if you tie in the stalk and wind that end in you tend to get a very bulky head because the stalk is quite thick). Tied in this way it makes for a stronger, neater fly. Tie in the hackle after it is wound where the body and hackle meet and carry the silk back through the hackle to the head. Wind a couple of turns of silk over the front fibres of the hackle so that they slope *slightly* backwards over the body; not too much though, otherwise they will not 'work' in the water.

Assuming that the creature we are attempting to imitate is in fact the spider, then it might be a good idea to build up a tag at the bend of the hook of either silver tinsel or, better still, polythene well soaked in varnish so that it becomes virtually transparent. This should then give the impression of the air bubble that the natural carries.

The Dressing (see Plate 5)
Silk: Sherry Spinner (brown)
Body: Bronze peacock herl
Hackle: Brown partridge
Hooks: 10 – 14 Old Numbers, down eye

BLACK AND PEACOCK SPIDER

As I said when writing of the Brown Spider, Tom Ivens was responsible for putting this fly before the angling public in his book *Still Water Fly-fishing*. It is certainly the most effective spider pattern used on the reservoirs. Again, it is one of those flies that catch fish for everyone but me! I do not think I have ever had a trout on it and I have used it many times because I felt if everyone else was getting results with it...

Method of tying

In Tom's original dressing he uses a black rib of tying silk and an underbody of floss silk to bulk out the peacock herl. As with other of his flies this one has been adulterated by the professional fly-dressers, and both these features are usually omitted. I frankly do not think these omissions make the slightest difference to the fish-taking potential of the fly but certainly the rib would mean that the fly would last longer after being 'got at' by a trout's teeth. Actually, of course, the body can be made much tougher by using the Walker method of winding the herl over a layer of wet varnish, and this is what I usually do.

Black and Peacock Spider

The silk is started at the eye and wound down the hook almost to the bend where a bunch of three or four strands of bronze peacock herl are tied in. Varnish is then run up the shank of the hook and the herl twisted together as in the Brown Spider and wound up the shank in the same manner. The ends of the herl are trimmed off and a longish-fibred black hen's hackle is tied in and wound in the normal way, the end of the hackle is tied in where the body and hackle meet and the silk carried back through the hackle to the head where the fibres are made to slope in the correct angle over the body of the fly. Whip-finish and varnish the head. Tom also has a tandem version of this fly which people tell me also takes fish – as I have said, I cannot speak from personal experience...

The Dressing (see Plate 5)
Silk:	Black
Body:	Bronze peacock herl over black floss if required
Rib:	Black tying silk if required
Hackle:	Dyed black hen's hackle
Hooks:	6 – 12 down eye, Old Numbers

ERIC'S BEETLE

One of my clients, Mr R. D. Stephens of Hatfield in Hertfordshire, asked me to tie some of this pattern up for him and since that time I have spoken to a couple of people who had bought some from him; they told me they had been very successful with it. I have not tried it myself but I have no doubt it will make a useful addition to your armoury of stillwater flies – although I believe that its inventor, Mr Eric Horsfall-Turner of Scarborough, used it originally as a river pattern. It is simply an ordinary Black and Peacock Spider with a fluorescent orange wool tag.

The Dressing (see Plate 6)
Silk:	Black
Tag:	Fluorescent orange wool
Body:	Bronze peacock herl
Hackle:	Black hen or cock
Hooks:	Short shank 8 – 14 down eye, Old Numbers

Eric's Beetle

BLACK SPIDER

This is another of the patterns I had not seen before 'Steve' (Mr R. D. Stephens) introduced me to them. I have even managed to extract a couple of trout on it from Blagdon, which for me and spider patterns (except the Brown Spider of course) is going some!

Method of tying

Run your silk down the hook from the eye to the bend and catch in a length of black chenille; the best way to tie this material in is to grip the very end of the fluffy 'rope' and with the nails of your forefinger and thumb slide the fibres off the centre core, leaving about a quarter of an inch clear of the fluff, and tie this piece of cotton in. By using this method you will avoid bulking up the back end of the fly. Wind the chenille up the shank almost to the head in even turns, tie in and trim. Then wind a hackle of black dyed hen in front of it and finish in the usual way.

The Dressing (see Plate 6)
Silk: Black
Body: Black chenille

145

Black Spider

Hackle: Black hen hackle
Hooks: 8 – 12 short shank, Old Numbers

LUREX SPIDER

On the infrequent occasions when I resort to more than one fly on my leader, the bob is quite often a Lurex Spider and this one really has caught quite a few fish for me. If I were using a two-dropper leader, the patterns I would choose might be something like this; on the point a Butcher or a Peter Ross, on the centre dropper a March Brown or a Wet Greenwell and on the 'bob' either the Lurex Spider or an Invicta, and any of those combinations would be pretty hard to beat. Mind you, I do not really feel very happy about using more than one fly at a time but when I do then these flies all do well for me. Once again it was Steve who brought this fly to my attention.

Method of tying
Wind your silk from the eye to the bend and then tie in a short tag of red fluorescent floss, wind the silk back up the body over the floss and trim off any surplus floss at the eye. This will ensure that you get an even body without a lump at the tail end; I know

Lurex Spider

it is a little more expensive on materials but it is worth it to get a good-looking fly, is it not?

Tie in a piece of flat silver Lurex at the eye and take this down the body to meet the mini-tail and then back up the body over the first layer to the eye where it is tied in and the end trimmed off. The ubiquitous hackle of black hen is tied in and wound in exactly the same way as for the previous three patterns.

The Dressing (see Plate 6)

Silk: Black
Tail: Red fluorescent floss silk
Body: Flat silver Lurex
Hackle: Black hen
Hooks: 8 – 12 down eye, Old Numbers

PARTRIDGE AND ORANGE

This is one of those famous North-country flies that are used extensively for upstream wet-fly-fishing for both trout and grayling. For some reason it went out of favour on the stillwater fisheries for a while but it now seems to be staging a revival. It has proved to be an extremely useful pattern for me, particularly in its smaller sizes.

I remember fishing at Clatworthy reservoir in Somerset some years ago; I was suffering one of those spells of 'short takes'; these come to all fly anglers every once in a while and an extremely frustrating experience they can be. Fish come at the fly, the take feels firm and then for no apparent reason the trout 'falls off'. Either that or you suffer a series of little tweaks and just cannot connect in the first place – either way it is enough to make you want to throw your rod at the fish! (I had a friend who actually did this – I noticed though that the rod he threw was an old battered job and not his brand new J. J. Triumph! Lacked conviction, I thought...)

I had tried almost everything short of a Mills Bomb to catch those darned fish, even a particularly vicious-looking Sweeney Todd with a flying treble out the back end, still nothing but tweaks and weak hook-holds. Finally I calmed down enough to start going through the fly-box in earnest to see what might interest the fish enough really to take it as though they meant it. I ended up with an assortment of flies that you would not believe, everything from nymphs and dry flies to streamers and big lures – nothing would they look at long enough really to grab hold. More in desperation than hope I tried a little size 16 Partridge and Orange, and straightaway I caught fish, all well hooked in the

Partridge and Orange

scissors. Not big fish, probably about the 10–12oz mark but nonetheless welcome after the frustrating time I had been going through; I did not catch all that many either, because as I started catching them so the rise slowly petered out. I think I wound up with four or five but at least my shattered self-confidence was restored, and confidence is always half the battle. The moral of that little story is that perseverance pays – even if it is only perseverance in trying enough flies until you come up with the right one . . .

Method of tying
Tie in the silk in the normal way but do not wind it down the hook shank; where the first half dozen or so turns of silk finish catch in a piece of bright orange floss silk. Run varnish onto the bare hook shank and wind the floss down the hook to the bend and then come back up the hook over the first layer and tie in and trim off the surplus where you first started winding it.

We now tie in a brown partridge back feather in exactly the same way as we did for the Brown Spider and wind a hackle in front of the body, make it fairly sparse, two turns at most. Make a neat whip finish keeping the head as small as you can, then run a couple of coats of varnish over the head.

The Dressing (see Plate 6)
Silk: Brown or orange
Body: Bright orange floss
Hackle: Brown partridge
Hooks: 12 – 16 down eye, Old Numbers

PENNELL'S CLARET AND THE BLACK PENNELL

As I said when writing of the Lurex Spider, I am not overfond of using droppers when I am reservoir-fishing; this is because of two main problems which can arise when more than one fly is used.

The first is the ever-present danger of having a hooked fish run you through a weed-bed, in which case a break is virtually guaranteed when the free fly (or flies) snags up.

My second objection is the possibility of hooking another fish

on the loose flies. Of course, it is perfectly possible to get away
with it and land both fish, but the odds against this are pretty
high. The common advice is that you should *always* net the
bottom fish first. Not me! I *always* net the *biggest* fish first!

However, none of these problems arise for the chap using one
fly. Certainly to anyone who has not had at least a season's experience of reservoir-fishing I should say, stick strictly to the singleton, it is a darned sight safer.

Multi-takes are fairly rare; it is perfectly possible to fish a team
of flies for years and not have it happen, then out of the blue it
crops up maybe three or four times in a season. The main problem
the beginner will experience (and this I *can* promise you) is that
there will be a devil of a lot of knot unpicking to do; you will be
up to your eyeballs in tangles. Whether it all seems worthwhile is
up to the individual but to those who think it is, these two flies
are dedicated.

The Pennell spider patterns can of course be effectively used
on their own, but without doubt their main use is as a top-dropper
or bob-fly. This is the one that everybody tells you will trip
lightly over the wave-tops and which the trout will find completely irresistible; it never quite works out that way for me (or

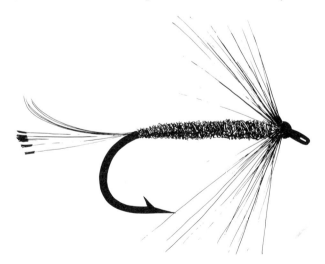

Pennell's Claret

anybody else I have seen trying it!). The darned things are always under the surface or flying around in mid-air. The only time I can achieve this 'tripping over the wave-tops' bit is when I am dapping; it works all right then. Folklore, I reckon.

Method of tying

We shall start with the fly I have found to be the more effective of these two, the Claret. Wind tying silk down to the bend of the hook and there catch in a bunch of tippet fibres and on top of these a golden pheasant crest. Also tie in the ribbing tinsel at this point. Carry the silk up the shank for three-quarters of its length, binding down the spare ends of these three materials as you go, trim off and wind the silk back to the bend. Dub on some seal's fur – you will find it easier if you have first waxed the tying silk because seal's fur is very springy stuff – and wind this up the shank to a point just beyond where you trimmed off the tails. Rib the body with neat even turns of tinsel and trim off. Now tie in a long-fibred furnace hackle by the stalk and, gripping the tip with your hackle pliers, wind on three or four turns, tie off at the back of the hackle and take the silk through it to the eye. Hold the fibres gently back with your left hand – I am assuming right

Black Pennell

through this book that the reader is right-handed, if not, then just reverse the instructions – so that they slope slightly back over the body and tie a neat head where the turns of silk press against the hackle to hold them in position.

I have never found that the Black Pennell has done as well for me as the Claret version. Funny, that; the Zulu has always been a fly I have done well with and that is pretty black. Still, I suppose it is like any other fly; if a pattern is successful for you, you use it more often; and you cannot catch fish on flies you are not using. Take the tying silk down the shank from eye to bend, tie in a piece of oval silver tinsel and wind this as a tag. You can use the same tail as for the Claret pattern if you wish but I prefer to use just the tippet fibres. Tie in the tail and bind down the ends as before, but do not carry the silk back down the shank again. Just behind the eye tie in a strand of black floss silk and wind this thinly down the shank and up again, and trim off the end where you first tied it in. Rib the body with the end of the piece of tinsel you used to make the tag, tie in and trim off the end.

A long-fibred black hackle is now tied in and wound as for the Pennell's Claret – if you decide to use the flies for dapping, it will pay to make it a thicker, stiffer and altogether bushier hackle than you would use on the normal wet pattern.

Right then, away you go – and do not say I didn't warn you about all those droppers!

The Dressings (see Plate 6)

Pennell's Claret

Silk:	Black or claret
Tail:	Golden pheasant crest and tippet
Rib:	Gold wire or oval gold
Body:	Claret seal's fur
Hackle:	Furnace cock

Black Pennell

Silk:	Black
Tag:	Oval silver tinsel
Tail:	G.P. tippet
Rib:	Oval silver tinsel

Body: Thin black floss silk
Hackle: Long black cock
Hooks for both patterns: 10 – 14 Old Numbers

ZULU

This is a fly that I have used with great personal success. I have had a lot of trout on it, both as a dropper fly and also on its own. Sometimes I even use it as a dry fly, almost as a sedge – stripped in fairly fast – and the trout come at it with great gusto. It also does very well as a grayling pattern on the chalk streams; in this case I am pretty sure it is the red tail that does it, grayling do seem to like a fly with a touch of red on it. Of course its main use is as a bob-fly on a two-dropper leader and this is where most people use it but I must say that I have found it more effective as the middle fly – still, that is probably just the peculiar way I fish . . .

There is another version of this fly, the Blue Zulu. I have never yet managed to catch a fish on it but I know that many anglers find it an effective pattern, and if you want to try it all you have to do is to substitute a blue hackle for the black one.

Method of tying
Wind the silk down the shank in the normal way and catch in a tail of either scarlet ibis substitute or scarlet wool – I prefer the ibis – after you have tied in the tail, catch in a piece of flat silver tinsel and bind down the spare ends of tail and tinsel as you did for the Pennell patterns. Take the silk back down the shank again to the tail and dub on the body material of either black wool or seal's fur. I normally use wool because sufficient sparkle is given to the fly with the hackle, and I see no point in using seal's fur and that filthy wax if I can avoid it; the wool is very easy to dub onto dry silk. Wind the dubbing up the body to just behind the eye. At this point tie in a long, short-fibred black cock hackle; dyed is generally better than natural, as the colour is deeper. Wind the hackle for two or three turns directly behind the eye to make the hackle denser at the front and then wind it in open turns, palmer-fashion, down the shank to the tail. Secure the hackle with the ribbing tinsel by winding it up the body through the hackle, going in the opposite spiral to that taken by the

Zulu

hackle. Tie in the tinsel at the eye, wind a small neat head of silk, make a good whip finish of at least four turns of silk and then varnish the head. On all the hackled wet flies there is no excuse for making the heads too big. They should be as small as possible; after all, there is no wing to tie in, is there?

The Dressing (see Plate 6)

Silk: Black
Tail: Scarlet ibis substitute or scarlet wool
Rib: Fine flat silver tinsel or Lurex
Body: Black wool or seal's fur
Hackle: Black cock
Hooks: 10 – 14 Old Numbers

SECTION FOUR

LURES

CHAPTER TEN

HAIR-WING LURES

SWEENEY TODD

Next to the Polystickle this must be Dick Walker's best known fly, and deservedly; the Sweeney Todd is a cracking pattern for reservoir use, it really does 'bring home the bacon'. It is one of my favourite stand-by flies. When all else fails, out comes that dear old lovable Sweeney, and it really is amazing just how often this pays off.

There seems to be a school of fly-fishermen in the UK which feels that for a lure to be effective it has to be stripped in at full throttle; in my experience this is seldom the case. A fairly slow, steady retrieve generally seems to do best for me with this particular fly. The thing to do, though, is to keep altering your rate and style of retrieve until you find the one that appeals to the fish on this particular day. For instance, it may be that long steady draws of the line with virtually no pause in between, are what the fish want. Or perhaps two fast short pulls with a long pause to let the lure sink down again may be effective. The fish may be feeding at any level, from a few inches under the surface to right on the bottom, and this is something the angler has to determine before he can really start to catch them. If a sinking line is used then the *only* really successful way of finding the fish is to time the 'drop' on your watch – and it can take far longer for a fly to reach the bottom that most people believe, even on a high-density line it can be *three or four minutes* before the fly is working deep enough to catch trout.

I find that the best thing to do is to let the fly sink for, say, a minute and then retrieve it. If it has not picked up any rubbish from the bottom, then on the next throw I give it ninety seconds, and so on, until I find the bottom, then I deduct a few seconds from the sinking time and I know that it is fishing just off the lake-bed. Of course if I pick up a fish at an intermediate depth then I fish at this depth, at least until there is no other response; then of course I begin experimenting again but I keep in mind the depth at which I had the fish so that I can return to it later on to see if perhaps the fish had merely moved out of the area temporarily. Many people have told me they were fishing 'the bottom' when their fly was in fact only five or six feet deep in thirty or forty feet of water – it can take a lot of time for the line to sink.

Most of the time, of course, it is not in the least necessary to fish a fly on the bottom at all, but it is as well to find out first just how deep the water is in front of you. It cannot hurt, and it does give you some idea of the lay-out 'down there'. You may find, for instance, that you drag up a few little bits of broken twig, in which case it is a fair bet that you are fishing over or at least near to an old submerged hedgerow or a sunken tree. This can be a good holding spot for fish but at the same time it tells you that there is possible danger; if a fish dives deep, he may well be heading for a hidden snag and you have to stop him reaching it. On the other hand, you may bring up a piece of weed with insect life of some kind on it which can suggest a change of fly pattern to try and simulate that insect. There is nothing to be lost – except maybe a fly or two in snags! – and a lot to be gained from finding out just what the bottom is like in your particular area. Anyway, it sounds far more impressive when someone asks what you are taking fish on and you can say 'So-and-so's Fancy, forty seconds down', it makes it look as if you *really* did know what you were doing!

The Sweeney Todd is a particularly effective fly if it is used in the evening, just before the evening rise starts. (If you have been fortunate enough to find an evening rise, there seems to have been a remarkable shortage of them lately.) It also seems to take a lot of fish during a heavy chop, especially in dirty, coloured water.

I have a feeling (although Dick did not tell me so) that this fly came into being as a variant of the Black Lure but dressed with the hair-wing. The same 'fly' was the inspiration of my Ace of Spades which is another extremely successful pattern for reservoirs.

Sweeney Todd

Method of tying

Start winding your tying silk at the eye and carry it in open turns to the bend of the hook. Tie in the ribbing tinsel and wind the silk back up the shank for about three-quarters of its length. Tie in a length of black floss silk – generally I use the stout floss for this pattern, as it saves a lot of winding. Wind the floss up and down the body until you get a nice carrot shape, tie off and trim at the point where you tied it in, and rib in smooth, even turns with the tinsel. It does not really matter how close or wide apart the turns of ribbing on a fly are – although on this fly, if it is tied on a size 8 long shank, I like to see about six or seven turns – the main thing is that they should be tight and even; nothing spoils a fly's appearance more than bad ribbing.

The next job is to wind on a collar of magenta DFM floss. This should be about an eighth of an inch long and should start close to where you finished with the floss and the ribbing. Magenta, incidentally, is a pale, washed-out claret, almost a pink.

Turn the fly over in the vice and tie in a false hackle of magenta cock, spread it well with your left thumb as you are tying it in. Turn the fly back the right way up in the vice. Cut off a fairly substantial amount of *dyed* black squirrel tail (I stress *dyed* because the natural black squirrel tail has greyish roots, and I always feel that the wing on this pattern should be as deep a black as you can make it). Make the wing a shade longer than the length of the fly body and tie the bunch of hair in on the top of the hook shank just as you would for a normal wet-fly wing. There is one very big difference, though – and I was fairly roundly condemned for omitting to mention this when I wrote about the Sweeney in my column – you *must* use locking turns of silk to hold this, or any other, hair wing in place. This is simply done by lifting *just the hair* after it has been tied in and taking two or three turns of silk round the roots of the hair, not the hook shank. The silk is then taken over these turns and round the hook as well to force the hair to take up its proper wing position, and the head is finished off with smooth turns of silk, a whip finish and several coats of varnish. I always feel that it is most important that the heads of lures should be as smooth and glossy as it is possible to make them. This is because the lures generally have larger, more pronounced heads – certainly this is true of the hair-winged patterns – than ordinary wet flies and they can look pretty awful if they are not smooth. Some people find that when dressing hair-wing flies it helps to dip the butts of the hair into an adhesive before tying them down. Certainly this would make for a stronger wing without any chance of the odd hair coming out but with the normal locking turns the hair is usually fixed pretty firmly anyway. The thing to remember is that it only needs one single hair to work its way out of a wing, and then the pressure on the other hairs is reduced by that amount and that wing will slowly but surely fall apart. Make the locking turns good and tight.

The Dressing (see Plate 6)

Silk:	Black
Rib:	Oval silver tinsel
Body:	Black stout floss silk
Collar:	Magenta daylight fluorescent floss silk or wool
Hackle:	Magenta cock hackle (Dick tells me that he now uses a crimson hackle on this pattern)
Wings:	Dyed black squirrel
Hooks:	6 – 10 Long shank, Old Numbers

CHURCH FRY

This fly is the invention of Northampton's Bob Church, one of our most knowledgeable and expert reservoir anglers. It is a good general hair-wing lure that catches fish for lots of anglers, its basic design is very similar to the Sweeney and the only real difference is the colour of the various materials.

When I have used this fly I have found that takes have usually been down deep when using a slow, crawling-along-the-bottom type of retrieve. It can pay to use either a keel hook or to try the Walker style of 'weedless' fly, which is a fly tied with a weighted back made up of two or three layers of lead strip tied in along the top of the shank. The dressing is then reversed so that the wing goes where the throat hackle would normally go and the hackle goes on the back of the hook. This means that under most circumstances the hook travels in an upside-down position and is therefore far less likely to catch up in snags or weeds. The hook-point is also protected from the snags to a certain extent by the stiffish hairs of the wing. If the fish are down really deep then this can be a very useful addition to the fly-fisherman's equipment.

Method of tying

You dress this pattern in exactly the same manner as the Sweeney Todd but substituting the different materials, eg where you tied in a black squirrel tail wing on the Sweeney Todd here you would use a wing of grey squirrel tail fibres and so on.

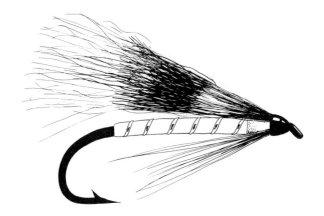

Church Fry

The Dressing (see Plate 6)

Silk: Orange or black
Rib: Flat silver tinsel or Lurex
Body: Orange floss silk
Collar: Magenta daylight fluorescent floss or wool
Hackle: A beard of orange cock
Wing: Grey squirrel tail
Hooks: 4 – 10 long shank, Old Numbers

FOURACRES' FANCY

Imagine if you would an opening day at Darwell reservoir in Sussex. Plenty of fish, beautiful surroundings and good company. Several of the lads from *Angling* magazine were there, and we spent more time chatting than fishing – nobody was frantic about catching fish, though we all wanted a few to start the season. If I remember correctly, both the editor and I finished with half a limit each, his was on a nymph and mine on the Ace of Spades.

The one member of the party to get his six-fish limit was Ron Fouracres, and he caught them one after another, immediately on moving into the spot I had just left. Still, he is such a nice chap you cannot hate him for very long! Anyway, that day he had collected an eyeful of lure (his own, not mine!) so he was more or less an invalid.

The interesting thing about his quick limit bag was the fly with which he did it: it had a body made from translucent green model-maker's fuel pipe, cut in half lengthways, then slid on the hook with the join at the belly and ribbed with black silk. It had a wing of grey squirrel tail fibres.

Not everybody has access to green fuel pipe, so when I came to tie some up I made a few variations, but the fish did not mind. It went down rather well at Weir Wood and really went like a bomb at the Draycote press day in 1971 . . .

I had been fishing nymphs and small wet flies for an hour or so with no response whatever from the fish, and it was only after this hour that I did the sensible thing: had a look at see what the trout might be feeding on. And there they were, hordes of sticklebacks. I had a quick look through my fly-box to find a likely imitation and caught sight of Fouracres' Fancy. There was just the one, and I remember thinking that if this *was* the one they wanted I hoped I would not lose it. So, third cast, I was into a lovely brownie of 2lb plus, and very soon three more fish followed it into the bag. Then I decided on a break.

Having watched all those other normally typewriter-bound journalists casting furiously, I decided it was about time I attended to my own business, went back to my pitch, took two more fish without much effort. Then a back cast dropped the fly into a tangle of grass and I broke off the fly on the forward punch. As I still wanted two more fish for my limit, I drove down to the fishing lodge, took out my portable fly-dressing kit and tied up six more copies. I went back and got my limit. A very handy thing, that kit...

Method of tying
The dressing I use is fairly simple. On a size 6 or 8 long-shank hook I wind black tying silk down the hook to the bend, there I tie in a short length of fine silver Lurex. I wind the silk back to the eye and tie in there some green Lurex strip, which is then wound down the shank to the bend and back to the eye again, where it is secured, and the end trimmed off.

The silver Lurex is now brought up as a rib, fairly well spaced, so that plenty of the green shows through. This is again tied off

Fouracres' Fancy

at the eye and trimmed. At the head a length of stretched polythene strip is tied in and wound back and forth over the body to
produce a neat carrot shape completely covering the Lurex. As
I wind, I apply plenty of cellulose varnish to the body, which not
only makes the polythene turn transparent but makes the fly
almost indestructible. It becomes completely solid. (Who said it's
now a plug?) Be careful, though, when the body gets fairly fat,
because the wet polythene tends to slide about a lot – care is
needed at this stage.

Now cut a substantial amount of fibres from a grey squirrel's
tail – the hair with the white tip. Its length should reach just past
the bend of the hook when tied in as a wing; not too long, otherwise fish are likely to strike at the white tip and miss the hook.

If you wish you can tie in a few hairs from a black dyed squirrel
tail on top of the grey fibres – I think it improves the appearance
of the fly, though whether the fish give a darn I have no way of
knowing. Do not forget those locking turns of silk round the
roots of the hair itself when you tie in the wing, otherwise the
fibres are liable to pull out and all you will have left is a green
body . . . It is next to impossible to get small neat heads on flies
when using a substantial amount of hair for a wing; hair does
not compress as well as feather. Do not worry too much about it
– the fish do not.

The Dressing (see Plate 6)

Silk:	Black
Rib:	Fine silver Lurex
Underbody:	Green Lurex
Body:	Stretched polythene, varnished
Wing:	Grey squirrel tail, with black over if required
Hooks:	Long shank 6 – 10, Old Numbers

WHISKEY FLY

This pattern must surely have been *the* success story of 1971–2.
Reports of large trout and large bags of trout came filtering in
from all directions; people were catching trout from all the
reservoirs on these flies. So, I reckon it is about time someone
published a description of the correct tying, and as far as I know

this *is* the first time; certainly it is the first occasion it has appeared in a book.

Method of tying

For this fly Albert Whillock (the inventor) does not use tying silk at all; all the finishing, whips and so forth are done with fluorescent nylon floss.

Fix a long-shank hook in the vice and get some of that silver or gold Sellotape that is sold in stationer's for wrapping Christmas parcels. Wind one turn of this round the bare shank leaving about an eighth of an inch gap at the bend; place the end of a piece of scarlet DRF nylon under the sticky tape and secure it by taking another turn of tape over it, trim the tape off square along the hook shank. Wind a neat, fairly long tag of the nylon behind the Sellotape and then come up over the body making an evenly spaced rib as you go. Run clear varnish over the whole body.

Reverse the fly in the vice and tie in a false hackle of hot-orange cock. Turn the fly the right way up again. Take a bunch of dyed hot-orange calf's tail fibres slightly longer than the hook and tie these in as a wing; you can, if you wish and if you have any, add a jungle cock eye feather either side of the wing. I myself do not think it is strictly necessary. Now a smooth head is built up of the fluorescent nylon and a whip finish is made and the end of the nylon trimmed off. The head is then varnished.

Just what a trout takes it for or why I shall probably never

Whiskey Fly

understand, a more unlikely-looking creature I never saw swimming about underwater, still, take it he does and that is what fishing is all about. I think perhaps it bears out my theory that lures are not taken in mistake for a small fish at all but purely because they are trespassing in the trout's immediate area and are therefore either a threat or a competitor.

The Dressing (see Plate 6)

Silk:	Scarlet fluorescent nylon floss
Body:	Gold or silver Sellotape. Varnished over body and rib
Tag:	DRF scarlet nylon floss
Rib:	As for tag
Hackle:	Hot-orange cock hackle
Wing:	Hot-orange calf's tail, with jungle cock eyes if required
Head:	As for tag
Hooks:	6 – 8 long shank, Old Numbers

CHAPTER ELEVEN

STREAMER FLIES

Six or seven years ago I received a letter from that well-known professional fly-dresser, Peter Deane of Eastbourne. It contained two very interesting flies, both streamers; flies designed by Lew Oatman, an American, to imitate small fish. They were in the streamer-fly tradition but they incorporated some unusual materials that attracted my eye. I used these two flies from time to time on lakes and reservoirs, and they accounted for some really good trout; I suppose I must have had a blind spot where these patterns were concerned for I never tied any for myself as stock flies. I just carried on using the two that Peter had sent me with the obvious result that eventually they were lost. So I had to bother Peter again; I asked him for the dressings so that I could pass the description on to you. Here is a passage from his letter:

> I am glad you had some success with the Lew Oatman Darters, and have much pleasure in sending you the dressings of both. The late Lew Oatman was an old friend of mine but died quite suddenly about five years ago. This was a great loss so far as American professional fly-dressers were concerned, as he was thought by many to be their best – Ray Bergman included. His best-known patterns were the Montana nymph and a special tying of the Coachman on a long-shank hook. His work was much acclaimed throughout the States, and *Esquire* magazine ran a feature about him just before he died.

A man I am sure whom many fly-dressers would have liked to meet; perhaps a little of the man's originality of thought will come across in my description of these two flies.

Oatman's Golden Darter

Method of tying

As the method of tying both patterns is similar I shall content myself with just telling you how I tie the Silver Darter. Use black tying silk and tie in at the head, carry the silk down the hook shank to the bend and there catch in two strips of fibres taken from a Lady Amherst pheasant tail. As with the ibis substitute feather used for the Butcher, these strips have an inbuilt tendency to curve. I therefore find it preferable to use the two strips to counteract the curve and give me a neat straight tail. The next item to fix in is the ribbing tinsel. The fine one is what is needed here; for the bodies I always use the Lurex which is 1/32nd of an inch wide, you cannot get a decent smooth body if you use the very narrow material. Carry the tying silk up towards the eye and tie in a length of white floss silk; take this down the body to the tail and then come back up over the first layer to the eye, tie in and cut. Two layers should be quite ample because we want the body to be nice and slim. The next thing is the ribbing; carry the Lurex up the body to the head; keep the turns evenly spaced and tight. (As I have said before, nothing spoils the look of a fly so much as uneven ribbing, so nice and even, *please.*)

Turn the fly over in the vice and tie in a false hackle of peacock sword feather fibres (take these from the tip of the feather where it becomes more dense). Half a dozen or so fibres should be enough. Make sure that the natural curve of the feather brings the tips up under the fly and not sticking out at odd angles. Turn the fly up the right way again and tie in four longish badger cock hackles as a wing – these should be at least twice as long as the hook. I find it best to make up the complete wing on the bench and tie it in as a whole, but it might be easier for some

Oatman's Silver Darter

people to tie in two hackles back to back and then a further two
on the outside of these; either way the result should be a neat,
strong wing, white with a deep black bar running down the
centre. The final part of the winging is the addition of jungle cock
eye feathers on either side.

Finally, make the head fairly long and slim, quite the reverse
of what is required when tying a salmon fly. Do a good whip
finish and varnish.

The Dressings

        Silver Darter *(see Plate 6)*

Silk:	Black
Tail:	Lady Amherst pheasant tail
Rib:	Fine flat silver tinsel or Lurex
Body:	White floss silk
Hackle:	Peacock sword feather
Wing:	Four badger cock hackles
Sides:	Jungle cock or substitute
Hooks:	2 – 10 long shank, Old Numbers

        Golden Darter

Silk:	Black
Tail:	Oak turkey wing strips
Rib:	Fine flat gold tinsel or Lurex
Body:	Yellow floss
Hackle:	Tips of starling breast feather
Wing:	Golden badger cock hackles
Sides:	Jungle cock
Hooks:	2 – 10 long shank

Lures

Over the last year or so I have been increasingly using the New Zealand style of winging lures, tying the wings down along the body as in the Matukas. Very successful they have been too. I like this method of winging because the wings do not wrap under the hook-points during casting, so making the fly swim lop-sided. This fly is an American streamer, and the wings are very liable to this unfortunate defect. It should perhaps be realised that this style of tying was invented primarily for trailing behind a boat or canoe on lakes and on the big steelhead rivers in the Western States, and since very little or no casting is required they work extremely well. They are tied to give the impression of a small fish, with long, mobile wings to give a lot of movement in the water.

Some of our British reservoirs are now allowing trolling between drifts or over selected areas of water (I use the term 'trolling' by the way because this is its most common name, although 'trailing' is the correct term) which in my opinion is a good thing. It is not a very inspiring method of fishing but it does provide a little interest on that long, hard pull up the reservoir. It is a bit of a bore when the drift down takes five minutes, yet the pull up-wind takes an hour into the teeth of a force-eight gale, so it is pleasant to think you will have the chance of a fish or two on the way back. It is the fellow who rows round and round trolling for hours on end who spoils things for others and causes this technique to be banned. He is just a damned nuisance.

I have found that to troll these streamer patterns correctly you have to use the line according to the prevailing conditions; in other words, if that gale I just mentioned is blowing then use a floating line because you will be moving quite slowly, and a sinker would just go straight down and you would pick up rubbish from the bottom. If it is only a freshish breeze then a slow sinker or a sink tip would be better. In a flat calm use a fast sinker. I seem to pick up most fish when the fly is fishing about three or four feet down. If you do decide to try this method make certain that the reel handle can revolve freely and that the check is as light as possible, otherwise thirty or forty pounds' worth of gear can be whipped over the side of the boat.

Of course streamer patterns can be quite successfully used for conventional casting if you are prepared at every third or fourth cast to unwrap that wing; you certainly will not catch a trout if you do not. It is often well worthwhile putting up with the inconvenience if the fly is the pattern that the fish want; generally speaking, though, these patterns were tied originally to be 'trolled' and here they are at their best.

Method of tying
Tying streamer flies is really quite simple, but you must be certain that the proportions are correct. They are nearly all tied on long-shank hooks so put one of those in the vice – a size 8, say – and starting the tying silk at the eye, carry it down to the bend of the hook and catch in a tail of several fibres of golden pheasant tippet. Take the silk back towards the eye over the surplus end of the tippet as you go to make certain the tail is really secure. Tie in a flat piece of silver Lurex tinsel and wind smooth, touching turns down to the tail and then up again almost to the eye of the hook. Tie in and cut off the spare end.

The wings are made up of four hackles tied in back to back as in the Oatman patterns. First match up a pair of light blue hackles and then place on the outside of these a pair of furnace feathers. It is best to take them from either side of the cape as opposed to the centre feathers. This is because the outside feathers have a natural curve which can be used to lay the wing low over the body. Saddle hackles are best from a top-quality cock cape.

If you have them, tie in two jungle cock eye feathers alongside

Spencer Bay Special

171

the wing. A light blue and a yellow hackle are now tied in in front of the wing and wound together to make a 'collar' hackle. With the forefinger and thumb of your left hand gently tease the hackle fibres back and wind the tying silk over the roots to hold them back slightly so that they lie over the wing. You do not want that hackle standing out at right angles as it would if you were tying a dry fly, the hackle has to have the correct angle to provide a 'good entry' into the water. Whip-finish the head and apply two or three coats of varnish.

The Dressing (see Plate 7)

Silk: Black
Tail: Golden pheasant tippet
Body: Flat silver tinsel or Lurex
Wing: Two light blue hackles, back to back; outside these, two furnace cock hackles
Sides: Jungle cock
Hackle: A yellow and a pale blue cock's hackle, wound together
Hooks: 6 – 10 long shank, Old Numbers

CHIEF NEEDABEH

Earlier in this book I wrote about the Parmachene Belle – without doubt one of the gayest and brightest creations the fly-dresser can tie, a real sparkler. Now we come to another bright one, again from America and again a real dazzler. The reason I like to carry a few of these rather gaudy flies in my box is because there are times when virtually nothing else will take fish; if you cannot produce a *really* bright fly and present it just right to the trout then you are going to go home clean. Such occasions do not occur very often, but when they do you are going to kick yourself if you cannot offer the fish what they want. Aside from all this, though, they *are* great fun to fish, because you see *all* the action.

Imagine a day when the fish were moving only for the first hour or two of light; perhaps you picked up a brace early on and then it all went dead. Now the reservoir is a flat calm with perhaps a very occasional rise. As the sun rises higher even that rare fish activity decreases until by noon you are casting to a flat, motionless sheet of water that looks as if it could never produce a fish. Your casting and your retrieving become erratic, your shoulder begins to ache, the boat seat is much harder than when you started and you seem to be sitting in a floating oven. Now is the time to stop, relax and take stock.

Let us have a look at your outfit; the normal 9ft odd reservoir casting pole, a fast-sinking line and a lure (you replaced the nymphs an hour before when the indifference of the fish became apparent), the leader is 10ft long tapering to a 7lb point. Everything looks alright, according to the 'book' in fact, for this type of occasion. So, why no fish? The lure is a dull one; this is one of the main reasons. A dull lure works fine in cold or coloured water, but they rarely seem to do so well when the water is clear and glass-like under a hot summer's sun. In the evening when the sun has almost reached the horizon, a dull lure can be just the thing, but not during the heat of the day. Right then, what are you going to do about it?

For a start you can change that line to either a full-floater or a sink-tip. I have observed that contrary to all the 'rules' the fish are not necessarily down deep under these conditions but cruising just a couple of feet under the surface – this is not of course an invariable rule, nothing to do with fishing ever can be, but it works often enough to be well worth a try under these conditions. Next, lengthen the leader to about 14ft unless you are using a sink-tip line; this will keep the surface wake of the retrieved line well away from the fly. Rub soft mud or detergent on the leader to make it sink and then tie on a *really* bright fly and cast a fairly long way. Now, do not mess about with pauses in the retrieve, just keep that fly coming back fast and steady. It should be fishing just a few inches under the surface. Fish out the cast right to the side of the boat; you will be amazed how far a fish will follow a gaudy fly. At Chew Valley lake once I had one that followed the fly so fast it hit the side of the boat with a real thump, he must have had quite a headache!

The retrieve is now smooth and steady. A vee-wake appears about 6ft behind the fly: do not alter the retrieve speed, just keep it coming. You need strong nerves for this game . . . The gap narrows between the fly and the fish. Suddenly there is a wrench on the rod-top and a heavy swirl 10 or 12yds from the boat, and you are into him.

This is perhaps the nearest we in the United Kingdom can get to the excruciating anticipation enjoyed by big-game anglers going after marlin or sailfish and watching them coming at the bait or lure. The same thrill is experienced when using a sedge pattern, but there you are usually casting to rising fish, and it is normally in the late afternoon or evening; with the flashy flies it is under a hot sun and you do not *really* expect to catch anything at all, so the thrill is that much greater when the unexpected happens.

Method of tying

The streamer patterns have an unfortunate habit of looking as if they were frightfully complicated and difficult to tie, and this puts a lot of fly-dressers off – there is no reason to be afraid of them at all they are all fairly easy. Fix your hook in the vice and give it a good testing by twanging it with the tip of your forefinger. If there is the slightest sign of distortion, *get rid of it* and put a new one in the vice. The hook is the most important part of your tackle and it *must* be a good one.

Run black tying silk down the shank to the bend where you wind close-butted turns of silk for about an eighth of an inch; close turns are needed, otherwise the tag will not sit neatly. Tie in a piece of oval silver tinsel and wind a neat tag. The best way of doing this is to start winding at the front of the close whipping

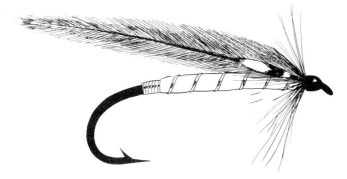

Chief Needabeh

and take the tinsel towards the bend and then back up over the first layer until you reach the point where you tied it in. Secure it there with the tying silk and leave the end hanging.

Run the tying silk back up the shank almost to the eye, allowing about a quarter of an inch on a size 8 long shank to receive the wing and the hackle. Tie in a piece of scarlet floss, wind a carrot-shaped body so that it meets the tag neatly without any over-lapping, finish winding at the eye end, tie in and trim off the surplus silk. Rib the body evenly with the tinsel you left hanging when the tag was finished. For the wings you will need four cock hackles about twice the length of the hook. Tie them in as you did for the Oatman patterns with the yellow pair in the middle and an orange pair on the outside. (How is that for brightness!) Tie in two jungle cock eye feathers either side of the wing, cover-ing at most a quarter of the wing's length. Now wind scarlet and yellow cock's hackles together in front of the wing; *do not* try to wind first one and then the other through the first. They must go on together so that the colours really mix and blend. Make a neat head, whip-finish and varnish.

The Dressing (see Plate 7)

Silk:	Black
Tag:	Oval silver tinsel
Rib:	As for tag
Body:	Scarlet floss silk
Wings:	Orange and yellow cock hackles
Sides:	Jungle cock eye feathers
Hackle:	Scarlet and yellow cock
Hooks:	6 – 10 long shank, Old Numbers

CHAPTER TWELVE

MATUKAS

GREY AND RED MATUKA

On a really scorching hot summer's day four or five years ago I sat in a boat by the dam at Weir Wood in Sussex. (In case you wonder why I keep mentioning this reservoir it is because it is my 'local', and I fish it more frequently than any other.) Fish? There did not seem to be one in the place, and now the hottest part of the afternoon was approaching. I was feeling a little despondent and I was getting darned uncomfortable.

With a jaundiced eye I peered at the fly-box in my lap and wondered if anything in there could possibly do the trick. I had been virtually through the lot and what I needed was something different. Approaching desperation, I tied on a Grey and Red Matuka that I had been meaning to try several times before. (This, incidentally is entirely the wrong time to try new flies, you ought to try them when the fish are feeding, otherwise you are not giving the flies a fair crack of the whip.) I had not the faintest idea how it was supposed to be fished – have you ever noticed how few books tell you actually *how to fish* the flies for which they give dressings? On a hot, cloudless afternoon in a flat calm anything was worth a try.

I cast into about a foot of water close up along the dam and began a long slowish retrieve. When the fly had travelled 10 or 12ft a small bow-wave began to follow it. I thought it was a perch – then I saw that pinkish flash of a rainbow's side as he sheered off. By now I was fishing in earnest and, using the same speed of retrieve I had three fish show in about ten minutes, but they would not take.

I tried slowing the retrieve right down, but this did not produce any interest at all. But when I speeded up the pulls until the fly was skipping through the water just under the surface things started to happen. I forget exactly how many fish I took that day; I have an idea it was about six or seven, but I do not think it was a limit. But not bad, not for an 'impossible' day.

Method of tying

To dress any of the following Matuka-style flies you will need long-shank hooks. For this particular one I like either a size 8 or a 6. Fix your hook in the vice and test it as I have described previously. Start the tying silk at the eye and carry it down the body to the bend, there you catch in a piece of oval silver tinsel and after teasing the end fibres off a piece of grey chenille you tie in the central core of cotton. Wind the chenille up the shank almost to the eye – it makes a lovely fat, furry body that sops up water like mad and so sinks very readily – tie in and trim off the surplus. Now reverse the fly in the vice and tie in a bunch of scarlet dyed cock hackle fibres as a beard or false hackle. Turn the fly the right way up again in the vice, ready to receive the wings.

Take two feathers from the body of a hen pheasant – the ordinary, common or garden one this time, none of your fancy stuff – and place them back to back with their tips absolutely level. Strip off most of the fibres on one side of each feather – strip the same length off as the length of the body – leaving just a few fibres at the tip on (what will be) the underside of the wing. Tie in the stalks at the hook eye so that the feathers stand up vertically along the body of the fly like a crest. Working from the tail end separate the fibres and rib towards the head with the tinsel. Do it carefully so that only the stalk is bound down on the top of

Grey and Red Matuka

the body, without pushing any of the fibres to the side. At first you will find it quite difficult to get an even rib, but as with most things practice is the only answer. Finish off the head neatly and apply varnish.

You can if you wish add jungle cock eyes to the sides of your Matukas – in which case they are called Imperials – but I have not found this to be really necessary. You could of course paint an eye on the head, a dab of white varnish with a black centre, that might help a bit. The thing is that now the import of jungle cock has been stopped I think it is better to save my small stock for flies that really need it.

It should not be thought that the Matukas will only take fish if they are stripped fast just under the surface; far from it, they are an extremely versatile lure and can be used at many different depths and speeds to good effect.

The Dressing (see Plate 7)

Silk:	Black
Rib:	Oval silver tinsel
Body:	Silver-grey chenille
Hackle:	A bunch of scarlet cock hackle fibres
Wing:	Hen pheasant body feather
Hooks:	6 – 10 long shank, Old Numbers

ACE OF SPADES

The Ace of Spades started off merely as a variation of the Black Lure, that most successful lure which is used very extensively, particularly early on in the season, on our reservoirs. It must have been about eighteen months or two years ago that I first started looking for something that would catch fish as effectively as the Black Lure but would not have its prime drawback – that unhappy knack of the wing twisting round under the hook-points during casting. This makes the fly swim in a lop-sided manner, and I can think of no occasion when I have caught fish on a fly that behaved in this way. Why that should be I cannot say; after all, it would seem reasonable at first glance that a fly swimming off balance like that would be taken for a wounded creature of some kind and as such would be liable to immediate attack by a predator such as a trout. This thinking, however, assumes that the trout takes a lure because it thinks of it as some kind of food, and I do not believe they do. All predators are very territorially minded; I incline towards the theory (as I have said previously) that a trout attacks a lure because it feels it is driving off a competitor, an interloper into its immediate territory.

This theory would mean that the fish would not probably be bothered to attack anything that had the appearance of being crippled. It would only go for the healthy, active and therefore threatening animal, hence the fact that very few trout are caught – in my experience, and I stand open to correction here – on flies that do not swim upright. Of course all this is mere theory and speculation but until I hear of anything which sounds like a more plausible hypothesis, I think I shall carry on with this one.

I am no great lover of lure-fishing in its commonly accepted sense, not, I hasten to add, because I think that lures as such are unsporting. It is simply because the normal method of fishing them bores me to tears. I am not keen on 'lure-stripping'; certainly it catches fish, even some big ones now and again but this high-speed retrieve is generally not for me. I will use this method on occasion if that is the only or the best way to catch trout, but as a general rule I like to use lures and that method of fishing them as an occasional armament, not as my main guns. If an angler does persist in lure-stripping on all occasions it can lead to a pretty thin time, particularly in the mid-summer months.

The first thing I had to come up with in my design for an 'anti-wing-twisting-type-of-black-lure' was a method to stop those wings 'getting at' the hook. The obvious solution was a hair-wing like Dick Walker's Sweeney Todd. The only snag with hair, as I saw it, was that it just was not dense enough. Sometimes there is no finer fly for taking trout than the Sweeney, I have particularly found this to be so in the evenings. For general daytime fishing, though, I needed something that gave a more solid silhouette than hair. It obviously needed to be feather but fixed in some way that would cure this twisted-wing business. After a little thought it became obvious that the only answer would be the Matuka style of dressing. I started work on perfecting a dressing that would appeal to both British anglers and British trout, this, rather than another general pattern that would have been useful to the New Zealanders who had invented this style of tying. (I have since received word that the Ace of Spades has done great things on Taupo, so perhaps trout really *are* the same the world over.)

I tried various combinations of materials that looked promising until I finally came up with the dressing that is now the Ace of Spades, with a black hen hackle wing and a 'roof' wing of dark bronze mallard feather over it. A silver rib and a few strands of guinea fowl hackle at the throat finished off the dressing. It looked as if it ought to catch fish – now to the acid test – I took the finished article down to Weir Wood and the results were extremely gratifying. In fact I fair hammered 'em!

Only last week I was down at Weir Wood again. I had a rather similar experience to that which I describe in the story of the Sinfoil's Fry; the trout were rising, solidly and consistently, and they were taking a minute smut, a little tiny fly that would have been virtually impossible to tie up as an imitation – size 30 hooks, would you believe! Anyway, it was far too small to compete with. With a feeling of frustration I decided that the only thing I could possibly do was to offer the trout a competitor as I had done with the Sinfoil's Fry, years before. I tied on an Ace of Spades, watched for the next rising fish, put the fly right in front of his nose, whipped it across fast and he was on . . . The rise stopped completely when I was at seven fish. It is strange how you feel slightly cheated when you cannot get that final one, no matter how hard you try. I do not mind catching a brace or two of fish in a day, that is fine, but once it gets past six I want to go all the way – trout are not the only funny animals. . .

Another interesting experience with this fly occurred down at Chew Valley Lake in Somerset. A southerly wind had been blowing at near gale-force for weeks and the only place where I or anyone else I spoke to had been taking fish had been on the Woodford Bank, which naturally – faces south. Casting into something that resembled a cross between Cape Horn on a bad day and the maelstrom was not only frustrating, it was a complete waste of time. Eventually we all went up to Woodford Lodge for a sandwich and a quick nip of the 'hard stuff'. I noticed after an hour or so that the wind had dropped slightly. I gathered myself and my belongings together and between the rain downpours I managed to extract three fish, all good rainbows of between three to four pounds. I am sure the only reason I caught those fish in that churned-up brown Windsor soup was because the Ace of Spades has such a dense silhouette. I gave several flies away to other anglers on the banks who asked the inevitable question, 'What'd he take?' Of the half-dozen anglers I gave flies to, everyone had at least one fish whereas the people who came along after stocks had run out had nothing. Almost exactly the same thing happened the following day but this time the conditions were a shade more reasonable – it was still blowing the same but the rain had decided that it would give us at least a short break. As far as I am aware the only fish taken on that bank on those two days fell to the Ace of Spades, and, they were nearly all good fish.

Method of tying

Fix a long-shank hook in your vice and after testing it for temper run your tying silk down it from the eye to the bend where you tie in a piece of oval silver tinsel as a rib. At the same point you tie in a piece of black chenille. Strip the fluffy fibres off as you did for the Grey and Red Matuka and tie in the core. Wind the chenille up the body almost to the eye, tie in and trim.

Choose two black dyed hen hackles that are about twice the length of the hook. Put them back to back so that the tips are perfectly even and then tear off about half the fibres on the underside. Tie in the stalks at the head and rib the body with the tinsel going through the fibres of hackle, binding this upright onto the body of the fly. Trim off the tinsel at the eye. Take two strips of

Ace of Spades

dark bronze mallard flank feather, about twice the width needed for the ordinary folded strip wings I described in the section on wet flies. These need to come from opposing feathers. Lay them one on top of the other, straighten them out as much as possible and then fold them over the black hackle wing and tie them in at the head, just as you would for an ordinary wing. Make sure these strips are not tied in too long, otherwise you will get the light-grey roots of the feather showing through and we want to keep the wing as dark as we can. They should completely enclose the underwing for about half its length.

Turn the fly over in the vice and tie in a short hackle of speckled guinea fowl hackle, not the wing feather, that clings together too much and the effect is too harsh. Turn the fly the right way up in the vice again and wind a neat, small head, whip-finish and apply at least three coats of a good quality varnish. Like any other fly the Ace of Spades is not always successful, but it does take far more than its fair share of fish – which I reckon is all you can ask of any fly.

The Dressing (see Plate 7)

Silk:	Black
Rib:	Oval silver tinsel
Body:	Black chenille
Wing:	Dyed black hen hackle tied as a crest
Overwing:	Bronze mallard, dark
Hackle:	Guinea fowl
Hooks:	6 – 12, long shank, Old Numbers

RED QUEEN

While the Ace of Spades is a drab pattern – purposely so – the Queen is, if not exactly bright, at least considerably more vivid in the winging feather. The method of fishing this pattern that I have found to be most effective is to use a floating line or a sink-tip and retrieve at a medium pace with slight pauses in between pulls; it does not seem to do very well when it is deep-sunk.

I have not had any large bags on this fly as yet. I have only been using it for about a season and a half and then not all that often; it has caught me two trout of over four pounds in that time though. Three of my readers wrote to tell me that they had enjoyed great sport with it down on the West Country lakes since I first wrote about it in my column in *Angling*.

What I wanted when I first tied the Red Queen was a pattern with similar attributes to the Ace of Spades but just that shade brighter. It took considerably more experimentation to find the right combination of materials than did the earlier fly.

Method of tying
Fix a long-shank hook into your vice and run either black or scarlet tying silk down the shank to just short of the bend, where you tie in a length of scarlet fluorescent floss silk and a bunch of peacock herl strands, four or five. Now take the tying silk back up

Red Queen

the shank almost to the eye. Twist the peacock herl together to form a 'rope', run varnish up the shank and wind the herl up the hook over the wet varnish. Tie in the herl and trim off the ends. Fix at this point, by their butts, two scarlet or crimson cock hackles, back to back, which have had most of the fibres stripped off underneath as we did for the other Matuka dressings. Do not compress any of the top fibres with the silk, otherwise they will stick out at odd angles and spoil the appearance of the finished fly.

Working from the tail end, separate the hackle-wing fibres by pushing them forward and rib the body with the floss silk; work your way slowly and carefully up the fly, binding down the wing as you go, keeping this ribbing as even as possible. Tie in the floss at the same point where you fixed the hackle butts. *Do not* cut off the end of the floss because you are now going to wind a 'collar' just in front of the wing. This is to make a bright 'striking point' for the fish, a similar idea to that of the Sweeney Todd. Wind several turns of the floss until you get a smooth collar of about an eighth of an inch long. Fold a single strip of bronze mallard over the wing and tie this in so that it encloses the 'crest' of hackle winging. Do not use the double layer of mallard as you did for the Ace of Spades; this fly wants a lighter, more ephemeral look to it. The mallard needs to be longer in this fly than in the other pattern, it does not matter if the lighter roots of the feather show – the grey part – so make it at least half as long again as the body.

Reverse the fly in the vice and tie in a beard hackle of a bunch of white cock hackle fibres. Turn the fly the right way up again in the vice and wind a neat smooth head, making it fairly long. If the silk you used is scarlet then you apply a coat or two of clear varnish and then a dot of black varnish for the eye on each side of the head, and finally run on another coat of varnish over the whole head. If you used black silk you will have to use scarlet varnish as a base colour, then carry on as above.

The Dressing (see Plate 7)

Silk:	Scarlet or black
Rib:	Scarlet fluorescent floss
Body:	Bronze peacock herl
Wings:	Two scarlet or crimson cock hackles
Collar:	Scarlet fluorescent floss
Overwing:	Bronze mallard strip
Hackle:	White cock
Head:	Scarlet with black eye
Hooks:	6 – 10 long-shank, Old Numbers

BLACK AND SILVER MATUKA

This fly came about through my messing about one day at the fly-tying bench. I was looking for new materials for winging the Matuka dressings. (I don't suppose for a moment that I am the first to have used this material for winging these flies, it just happened to be 'new' to me.) I came across a couple of silver pheasant wings and the resulting pattern looked so attractive I stuck one in my box for a future trial. The trout liked it too, and it caught three limit bags for me under very difficult conditions indeed. It never fails to amaze me just what will appeal to a trout's fancy. The wing on this fly is very large indeed and it is impossible to avoid this because the feather is so wide. I cannot achieve my normally slim wing with this pattern but the fish do not seem to care. It almost makes me wonder if all my theories are wrong after all.

I well remember I was training a young lady once to be a fly-dresser. She had become quite a good tyer and was beginning to supply me with saleable flies; one day I asked her to tie up some Woodcock and Greens for me. She must have had a brainstorm because the wings were terrible; I wrote the batch off and tied some more up for the order myself. These revolting-looking flies went into the 'junk' box, and it was only after about another two years that I decided a clear-out was due. A local tackle-dealer wanted a job-lot of flies, any old rubbish, he said, so that the kids could buy them cheaply and strip off the dressings for the sake of the hooks. I sold him all the rubbish I could find; apparently he cheated a bit and put anything that looked reasonable to him into his stock boxes, at full price, I might add!

The upshot of it was that about a week later I received a frantic telephone call asking me to supply some of 'Those green jobs with the big wings'. They had sold like hot cakes apparently, and later he told me that several people had reported good catches on them – makes you think, doesn't it?

Method of tying
This fly is tied in an exactly similar fashion to all the foregoing

Black and Silver Matuka

Matukas – except that it is generally a lot simpler, with fewer materials – so it would be pointless my going through the same methods of tying again. Tie it just like the Grey and Red Matuka to the dressing given below.

The Dressing (see Plate 7)
Silk: Black
Rib: Oval silver tinsel
Body: Black chenille
Wings: Silver pheasant
Hackle: Magenta cock
Hooks: 6 – 8 long shank, Old Numbers

MATUKA BADGER LURE

I have a customer who each year orders a couple of dozen Badger Lures from me. He likes them tied on long-shank single hooks so really they become a streamer pattern. After I had made up my customer's regular order, I decided to see what this fly looked like as a Matuka. It looked good, I enclosed the one I had tied as a present with the 'streamer' tyings and tied up half a dozen for myself. The only remarkable happening with this particular fly was an occasion on a small Hampshire lake, I had no less than four trout take it on consecutive casts.

As with the Black and Silver Matuka there is no point in going right through the basic principles of tying this fly. The only remarkable things about it are the body which is of fluorescent orange wool, and the fact that short jungle cock eyes are tied in each side of the wing. It is a fly that could be well worth trying on those dour afternoons when conditions are hot and sultry, because that body is very bright indeed.

I should be very pleased to see more British fly anglers using the Matuka dressings. The ones which I have listed here and the standard New Zealand patterns will all take fish, and there is something much more satisfying about taking trout on a single hook rather than on the multi-hook rigs. Quite frankly, I can see very little point in using more than the one hook, particularly if it is a long-shank one; most of the time any trout I have taken on tandem hooks has been on the rear one and a single long-shank

Matuka Badger Lure

would have been just as effective without involving me in the risk of that fatal weak link, the joint between the hooks. I would finish by saying that they really are worth a trial and after just a little practice the winging is not at all difficult.

The Dressing (see Plate 7)
Silk: Orange
Rib: Oval silver tinsel, fine
Body: Fluorescent orange wool
Wings: Two badger cock hackles
Sides: Jungle cock, tied short
Hackle: Hot orange cock
Hooks: 6 – 10 long shank, Old Numbers

CHAPTER THIRTEEN

MULTI-HOOK LURES

BLACK LURE

As I have stated previously in this book, I am no great lover of lure-fishing. I have got nothing against lures as such, it is merely the indiscriminate use of them on all occasions to which I object. If other people feel that this is how they want to fish them, that is up to the individual – just do not expect me to join them; there is too much fun to be had from other forms of fly-fishing. I shall use the lure when I think it is necessary; I can even quite enjoy an hour or two's stripping (lures, that is!) but I am darned if I want to stand up to my thighs in water making them hurtle along all day. It is hardly the subtle approach, is it?

My main objection to tandem hooks – aside from that wing tucking itself under the hook-points every other cast – is that *weak link,* no matter how strong that junction may appear there is always the danger that it may weaken through the tremendous stresses imposed on it during casting. A trout's teeth can also fray the link if it is made of nylon, and wire joins like twisted Alasticum are completely hopeless because of that constant bending caused during the long-distance casting that is usually involved when using these flies; it sets up metal fatigue very quickly.

The main snag with lure-fishing is the attitude it seems to engender in the people who fish in no other way – this is the 'fish at any price' point of view, and I want no part of that. I am like any other angler, I thoroughly enjoy catching a good bag of fish but I want those fish to have been caught by using an intelligent approach and not by the mindless application of just one method. I should now like to give you an instance of what I am talking about.

About three years ago I was staying at a pub near to Chew Valley lake and the landlord introduced me to the 'expert'. This was a fellow who boasted that he 'never failed to catch trout at Chew'. I have no way of knowing how true that statement was but while I was there for my usual three days he came in with a limit bag each evening. His attitude was the 'fishmonger complex' carried to extremes. The sport aspect of angling seemed to elude him completely, he had no fun out of his fishing; he made it into a second job, designed to pay for his holiday. (All his catch was frozen and then sold in a market. I have no objection to people selling their catch but this chap was making a business out of it. I have even swapped the odd trout for a good dinner at an hotel myself but that I think is slightly different.)

Out of curiosity I went one day and watched him at 'work'. The three-hook black lure hurtled out about thirty-five yards, was allowed to sink and then frantically stripped back in at a very high speed indeed. He had two fish while I watched and these were thrown up the bank to die a lingering death without the courtesy of a blow from a priest, the hooks were literally ripped out. You see, it was all a question of speed, like being on a production line – and no time could be spared for the non-essentials. The whole thing might have been happening on a North Sea trawler rather than a reservoir bank. It was sickening.

As I have said, I am just like anybody else. It is very pleasant to take an occasional limit of trout, but a day can still be a successful one even if only a fish or two are the result. I should not want to make it part of my work – apart from my work as an angling journalist of course – the two things are separate and distinct from each other, and I go fishing to relax and enjoy myself. Lure-stripping all day long is hardly my idea of relaxation. A lure *can* be fished in other ways and, generally speaking, it will catch as many if not more fish than the really fast retrieve. It can be worked slowly along the bottom and perhaps take the bigger trout that will not look at a smaller fly. It can be used to simulate a wounded fish and catch trout as it sinks slowly after the coarse fish fry have been under attack and siege by the 'sticklebackers'. It can also be used as an 'irritant' as I have often used the Ace of Spades when the fish are feeding on a really small food-form.

The lure does not necessarily have to be retrieved at a high rate of knots to be effective although this is another of its uses – on occasion. I find the high-speed retrieve handy early in the season when the winds blow chill and I want some form of exercise to keep me warm, at least it means that you are constantly recasting. It can also be a handy method to have up one's sleeve, when, on a hot summer's day with a flat calm, it can sometimes catch fish that would not be caught by any other method; in my experience the fish that usually falls for this ploy is the rainbow – I reckon they are a little bit dafter than our native brownies . . .

Most lures are comparatively easy to tie as they do not have wings in the sense that wet and dry flies have them. The wings are usually made of hackles, not the web of birds' primary feathers, which are always more difficult to tie in. A lot of anglers do not realise, however, that although the lures are fairly simple patterns, for the professional fly-dresser they are highly uncommercial to produce. This is because making the mount takes so much time – that is if it is done properly. It is only too easy to turn out lures that look great, until they are used. The most important thing of all is that junction between the hooks; if this is not fixed properly and securely then as soon as a fish is hooked the lure will disintegrate. Any decently made lure will *have* to cost the angler at least three or four times as much as a wet fly. In professional fly-dressing the prime expense factor is time, and lures consume more of this than any fly other than the big, fully-dressed salmon patterns. It is nothing to spend ten minutes making up a simple lure whereas the winged wet flies, Peter Ross, Mallard and Claret etc, will only take between two to three minutes. So spare a thought for the poor pro' fly-tyer when next you have to pay the asking price for that big, three-hook lure.

The Black Lure is without doubt the most popular lure in use in Britain today: it is also (perhaps because it *is* the most popular and therefore is used more often!) the most effective. People have advanced theories that it simulates a leech, but I feel that it has a silhouette which is fish-shaped, and that is what accounts for most of its success. Whoever saw a leech moving through the water at the speed at which the Black Lure is commonly retrieved? I think that this pattern is the prime example of the aggressive instinct being triggered in trout; they attack the lure as a competitor, not as a food item.

Method of tying

The first job you have to do when tying up any lure is to make the mount. Two or more hooks have to be joined together in such a way that they will not come apart when very heavy stresses are applied to them – that is not easy. I have tried various methods, none of which have proved to be completely satisfactory, but perhaps the least bad has been to have a link of nylon mono-filament of 12 to 14lb b.s. The rear hook is set in the vice and the tying silk started at the eye (I often snip off the eye with pliers to make the finished fly neater) and wound about a third of the way

Black Lure

down the shank. The piece of monofil is squeezed gently in the tip of the pliers to serrate it – be careful that no more than half the length of the hook is scored in this way, otherwise the joint will be weakened. Lay the nylon along the shank and bind it down with close turns of the silk; the surplus end should hang off the back of the hook. Take the silk right down to the bend. The nylon is then brought up the shank to the eye and the silk carried up the shank again binding down the two sections of monofil so that they lie along-side of each other. The surplus end is now left hanging out over the eye. Make a good whip finish and trim off the silk.

Set the forward hook in the vice and, starting the tying silk at the eye, bind down in close turns to the bend. There you lay the rear hook and the monofil in place – make certain they are straight – and then bind over the nylon up to the eye again. Trim off the nylon so that there is a bare hook-length left sticking out in front of the eye. Score the tip of this with the pliers and bend the nylon back along the shank so that it lies snug up against the first piece and then bind it in tightly with the silk, right down to the bend. Whip-finish at the bend and trim off the silk. To make the nylon really secure you should now coat the silk with a good, powerful adhesive such as Araldite, but it is doubtful if it will ever pull out, even if varnish is used – I have *never* had one pull out, but I *have* had the link snap in the middle, that is where the real weakness lies, not in the tying. There is a variation on this method of making links and that is to use plaited nylon of about 6lbs b.s., this means that the link is more flexible and will stand up to casting strains better, it should also be about a third stronger. It does however have one main disadvantage; it bulks up the hook-shank so that the dressing is bigger, and of course it is also uneven due to the ridging of the plaited material. However, I mention it for those who have trouble with the strength of their links. One thing you should *always* do after taking a fish on a multi-hook lure and that is to check that link for signs of fraying, *it really is most important.*

After the mounts have had a good time to dry – say twenty-four hours – we can get on with the dressings. Tie the rear hook first. Start at the eye – if the hook still has one and you have not trimmed it off as I do – and carry the silk down to the bend in open turns and catch in a length of oval silver tinsel. The silk is then wound back to the eye and a length of fine black floss is tied in. This is then wound down the body to the bend and then back again over the first layer to the eye where it is then tied in and trimmed. The body is then ribbed with the tinsel – five or six evenly spaced turns are ample – tie in and trim, finish with a good, solid whip. Repeat this procedure on the front hook, and you are now ready to tie in the wings. You will find that a much denser wing results if dyed hen hackles are used rather than those from a cock cape. I also get much better results with a Black Lure if the wings are tied in alongside the hooks rather than being set over the top of the 'fly'; it is quite easy to achieve this effect but as with all things in fly-dressing it does need a certain amount of practice to get the wings set exactly right. It can sometimes pay to use four hackles for the wings on this fly as opposed to two – denser again – and people often find that if a jungle cock eye feather is tied in short alongside each side of the wing they get better results.

The Dressing (see Plate 7)

Silk: Black
Ribs: Oval silver tinsel
Bodies: Black floss
Wings: Black dyed hen hackles
Sides: Jungle cock if required
Hooks: 6 – 12, two or more tied in tandem, Old Numbers

WHITE LURE

Although the black pattern is without doubt the most popular of the lures, this one can sometimes be far more effective, particularly if the trout are 'sticklebacking'. More often than not this attack on small fish in the shallows is not conducted against the stickleback at all, it is the roach or perch fry the trout are after, and this lure is excellent at these times.

I have found, over many years of trial and error, that the best way to take trout on these occasions, is not to watch for fish, cast to them and then retrieve the fly fast as if it were a frightened fry. This is the normal approach, and I am inclined to believe that this is why a lot of anglers have a frustrating time with the fry feeders. I am convinced – as I said in the chapter on wet flies – that the trout are attacking the fish fry en masse and their turning and sweeping through the shoals damage the delicate bodies of the fry so that they can return later and clear up the casualties at their leisure.

To be used to its maximum potential at these times I believe the lure should be cast to the approximate area of the attack, allowed to sink under its own weight and then to lie on the bottom for a minute or more. When the retrieve is started it should be a very slow one, first of all a few twitches at the fly, then a little spurt or two of three or four inches in length and then, if there is no response from the trout a slow gathering-in momentum of the fly's movement until at the last it is being retrieved in the normal manner. This fairly complicated-sounding form of retrieve is designed to simulate the damage to and the slow recovery from the trout's attack. It can be extremely deadly, the only problem being on those waters that have a population of perch – they like it just as much as the trout!

The method of tying this lure is exactly the same as that used for the Black Lure except that white floss silk and white hackle wings are substituted for the black. The ribbing material is the same. Sometimes people do well with a White Lure tied up with a silver tinsel or Lurex body, but I have found that this particular pattern does best for me.

The Dressing (see Plate 7)

Silk: White or olive
Ribs: Oval silver tinsel
Bodies: White floss
Wings: White hen or cock's hackles
Hooks: 6 – 12, two or more tied in tandem, Old Numbers

CHAPTER FOURTEEN

POLYTHENE LURES

SINFOIL'S FRY

Since I first wrote about Sinfoil's Fry there have been many experiments and developments in man-made fly-dressing materials: polythene, plastic raffia (Raffine), plastazote, expanded polyethylene, and several others. Some of the patterns that have emerged have been strange indeed; I am inclined to think that no better imitation of a young fry (from a trout's point of view) has as yet shown up than that invented by my good friend Ken Sinfoil, head bailiff at Weir Wood reservoir.

Of course, as with any other fly that is given sufficient publicity, it tended, in the early stages to be thrashed to death; everybody had either a Sinfoil's Fry or a Polystickle (which was developed by Dick Walker from the article I wrote about the Fry in one of the weekly angling papers) on their leader. This was never our intention. We wanted anglers to use these flies at the appropriate time and not to look on them as the be-all and end-all of reservoir fly-fishing, which of course they are not. They are, however, most efficient fish-takers when the sticklebacks or the perch fry are about.

Just to be difficult, I am now going to tell you about an occasion when I had great success with Sinfoil's Fry when the trout were not interested in either fry or sticklebacks in the least!

I arrived at Weir Wood at first light on a summer's morning some years ago. I had the place to myself. I rowed on silk-smooth water, heading for Admiral's Wood, every couple of strokes I paused and looked over my shoulder to see if any fish were moving.

I suppose I was about halfway up the reservoir when I saw something that completely astonished me – a field where the water ought to have been . . . There it was, large as life, a brown-green field that stretched from bank to bank in the misty half-light; this demanded immediate investigation. The boat drifted gently along until I could see that what had looked exactly like a field was in fact floating algae. The peculiar thing was that it stopped dead in a straight line, and hardly a strand overlapped the invisible demarcation line. This was most peculiar, I had certainly never seen anything quite like it before; it was just as though a rope had been floated across the surface to stop the algae drifting. I imagine that what had actually happened was that the algae had floated up from the bottom on the previous day and an easterly wind had pushed them as far up the reservoir as they could go and then the massed plant-forms had clung together.

I saw that, suspended and caught in those algae, were million upon million of *Caenis* (the 'angler's curse') and the trout were having a field day, rises everywhere, but what could possibly compete with this banquet? A small Grey Duster is a fair imitation of the *Caenis,* but not when there were as many of them as this on the water.

So, what to do? I reckoned the only chance was a complete contrast, a competitor for the trout, a Sinfoil's Fry. And it worked, it worked beautifully. I saw a fish rising gently in the mass of green strands, sipping in the small insects, cruising along, concerned only with filling his belly to bursting point. A cast across his bows using a floating line and with the leader greased to within 18in of the fly; a stop-start retrieve as though the Fry was taking the fly as well, and the trout could not stand it! I had a limit of fish in under half an hour. Just an accurate cast and the correct fly, and I was home and dry. Easy. (It also meant that I had to stop fishing at 6.30 am, incidentally.) The one thing it did

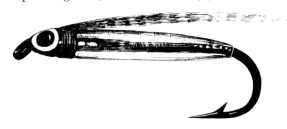

Sinfoil's Fry

prove was that a little thought with regard to the fly you use can pay off in a big way. I am convinced in my own mind that I could have flogged away all day with an imitation of the fly that was on the water and got precisely nowhere. The 'fly' I chose provided an annoyance factor to the fish, it also meant competition. Fish do not like competitors, at least not the predators like trout, so the fly gets taken and so incidentally does the fish!

Method of tying

When I tie the Sinfoil's Fry I always use long-shanked hooks, as the long shape gives a better imitation of a small fish. A bronze size 10 is fine. Tie in the silk at the eye and then immediately tie in a piece of flat silver tinsel, wind this halfway down the shank and then come back up over the first layer and tie in at the eye, trim off the surplus.

Take a strip of polythene about a quarter of an inch wide, stretch it gently between your hands. It should stretch to about three or four times its previous length and it also – strangely enough – becomes considerably stronger. I suppose some technical type will say that it's the molecules stretching and laying in line or something – I wouldn't know, I'm only a simple soul who was duly surprised when it *did* in fact become stronger! Tie the strip in at the eye and wind it up and down the shank until you have built up a smooth carrot-shape. Leave about a quarter of an inch clear of polythene at the eye, tie in and cut.

Fix a piece of scarlet floss to the hook and wind this in front of the body to form a collar. Scarlet fluorescent floss works even better, I have since discovered. You now shape the head with the tying silk, but be careful because just before the final layer or two of silk is wound you have to tie in a strip of feather taken from the 'bad' side of a bronze mallard feather, the part you would normally throw away. This *is not* a wing, it is there merely to give the fly a little movement, and it should be tied to lie low over the body and be *very slim* and tapered. Now wind on the last layers of silk, whip-finish and varnish. The head should take up about a fifth of the hook's length, as when you look at a young fry in profile it appears to be nearly all head, at least that is the most prominent part. If you wish you can add eyes by the simple expedient of painting on a dab of white varnish with a dot of black varnish as a pupil. I am pretty sure that eyes help.

The Dressing (see Plate 7)

Silk:	Black
Underbody:	Flat silver tinsel or Lurex
Body covering:	Stretched polythene strip
Collar:	Scarlet floss silk or fluorescent floss
Back:	Bronze mallard, the 'bad' side
Eyes:	White varnish, black varnish
Hooks:	8 – 14 long shank, bronzed, Old Numbers

GRAFHAM POLYSTICKLE

When Dick Walker invented this fly after reading my article about Sinfoil's Fry he had already been conducting numerous experiments with different body materials, trying to find something that would give the effect of transparency to his imitations of sticklebacks and small coarse fish. Stretched polythene provided the ideal solution.

I have found that the Polystickle (particularly the version which Dick named the 'Grafham Polystickle', I very rarely use any of the many variations these days) is without doubt at its most devastatingly effective when use over sticklebacking trout. I mentioned the type of retrieve I used for this type of pattern when writing of the White Lure, the same thing applies here except that this direct imitation of a young fish is even more effective. The trout you can catch by using this cast, letting it lie and then recovering at a slowly gathering speed, can be enormous. It is usually the big fellows who need a more substantial meal than their smaller brethren, who conduct these raids into the shallows. Too often you see anglers trying to cast across the path of a sticklebacking trout and missing out completely. I would usually try the very slow retrieve first and only if it fails would I then go on to the 'panicky fry' retrieve. This method is worth trying a considerable period after sticklebackers finish their main activity because when a trout's appetite is virtually satiated he will sometimes have a go at a fast-moving fry; I think he does this purely for the sport of it. Many is the time I have had a good bag of fish when they had been on the fry and then the action had virtually ceased except for one big fish. If I have been fortunate enough to catch him, his belly is almost always stuffed to bursting point with small fish – as I said, sport.

When the lake is a flat calm and there is no fish activity to be seen, there may well be the odd fish interested in feeding but only deep down. Put up a sinking line, cast well out and time the sinking of the line on your watch; then start a fairly fast smooth retrieve, and you may well pick up a good fish or two. For heaven's sake, though, do not use light leaders: 7–8lb b.s. is the very lightest I would use under these conditions because the takes are usually very hard and they are also difficult to anticipate.

Method of tying
Wax the first couple of inches of your tying silk and, starting at the bend of the hook, take several turns of close-butted silk to give a foundation for the Raffine back and tail. Take a piece of the Raffine about two or three inches long and tie it in so that it stands up vertically on the shank, half an inch or so should jut out past the bend of the hook. Take several *tight* turns of silk over this to hold it really firmly, as it is going to be under considerable pressure later on in the dressing.

Wind the silk in even, open turns to the eye. Stretch a piece of polythene in just the same way that you did for the Sinfoil's Fry. Tie in the stretched polythene about a quarter of the way down the shank; if you want a transparent body, all you have to do is to run a little cellulose varnish on before winding the polythene;

Grafham Polystickle

it is then wound up and down the shank until a fish-like shape is achieved, adding varnish as you go. When this sets, the body is virtually solid and almost indestructible. There is scope to vary the amount of transparency by adding the varnish to only the first few layers of polythene or to none of them, or of course you can use the varnish right through the winding. It depends which waters the fly is used on, and also on the light conditions, as to which will prove most successful; I find it best to carry a few of each type in my box.

Once the body is satisfactorily wound you tie in a piece of scarlet floss silk and wind this in front of the body as a collar. Reverse the fly in the vice and tie in a throat hackle of spread hot-orange cock hackle fibres, do not make this hackle too long, about a quarter of the body length is right. Turn the fly back the right way up in the vice and after thoroughly wetting the Raffine pull it really taut over the back and fasten it at the head with several tight turns of silk. Wind on a neat, smooth head of silk and make a whip finish of at least four turns. Apply varnish to the head until it is smooth and shiny. One tip here, the Raffine is extremely delicate, and after wetting it does tend to crinkle up, no matter how tightly it was stretched during the tying; I usually apply a final coat of varnish over the entire back as well as the head, this then holds everything firmly in place. Dick feels that the varnish (I usually use polyurethane, by the way) makes the back lose a certain amount of the translucency which it gains from being immersed in water. I really do not think it makes a halfpenny-worth of difference, and my main reason for using the varnish is to stop that Raffine back from crinkling up. This material is extremely difficult to work with and the sooner someone comes up with a decent alternative the better!

The Dressing (see Plate 7)

Silk:	Black
Tail and Back:	Brown Raffine
Body:	Stretched polythene
Collar:	Scarlet floss silk
Hackle:	Hot-orange cock
Hooks:	6 – 8 long shank, silvered, Old Numbers

CHAPTER FIFTEEN

UNCLASSIFIABLE PATTERNS

MUDDLER MINNOW

Trout enjoy proving me wrong! I should like to quote two in-
stances of this; if nothing else they prove that trout read the
very best angling magazines! For a start let us look at the fly we
are discussing here, the Muddler. For my first half-dozen or so
outings at the beginning of the 1972 season I could do no wrong
with the Muddler; this was particularly true at Weir Wood. I
would arrive there early in the morning, take out a boat and go
rowing off up the reservoir. When I reached a likely-looking spot,
out would go a Muddler and within a dozen or so casts in would
come a trout – invariably a brownie – the rainbows just did not
seem to want to know this particular pattern. I would go on like
this until I had got a comfortable two brace under my belt and
then I would begin experimenting with other flies to try and fill
out my limit; it all became quite routine . . .

Then one day I took my friend Tony Claydon out with me on
his second fly-fishing trip. 'Tony', said I, 'these Muddler Min-
nows are a damned good fly but I cannot catch anything but
brownies on them, funny that.' At the precise moment I uttered
those fateful words a fish grabbed hold of my fly down in those
murky depths, a second after that the water exploded as a nice
rainbow erupted from them. It is even worse if I make a dogmatic statement in print . . .

Take for instance the article I wrote about my series of nymphs
in *Angling*. I came right out with it and said that 'Of all the shades
of material that the fly-dresser uses, I have found over the years
that bright greens are the least effective.' What is wrong with
that, you may well ask? Well, I shall tell you. Those darned fish
had obviously read that Collyer-type-asking-for-it statement,
they read it and then quite cold-bloodedly set about proving me

wrong! No sooner had I said those words than the opening-day trip to Darwell was arranged, and whom should we meet there but Ron Fouracres, along with his 'Fancy' which naturally had a brilliant green body and which the trout just loved. I would advise any reader to think deeply and speak slowly when about to pontificate on either fly-dressing or fly-fishing – you never know who is listening.

Generally speaking, I have done best with the Muddler Minnow when fishing it deep down on a sinking line; again this technique calls for the use of your wrist-watch to time the 'drop'. This is most important as I have explained previously, it is no good going by guesswork. If you just let it sink and then haul it back in and you get a fish, you want to know the approximate depth at which that fish was swimming; this is because if one fish finds that depth a good, comfortable one and also is prepared to feed, then the odds are that there are other fish at that depth, and you can probably interest them also in your offering. As with any other sport or pastime fly-fishing does require a considerable amount of work to be put into it before the angler can hope to come up with fairly consistent results. *Nobody* expects to go out on a golf-course for the first time and do a Tony Jacklin, but the unhappy fact is that people *do* think that merely by throwing a fly at a stretch of water they are going to catch fish. Just as it takes time, practice and expertise to perfect a golf-swing, exactly the same requirements are needed to be successful at fishing. To get to be good you have to work at it. That little tip about timing the sinking of a line can be of great help in getting consistent results.

I like, where possible, to have this fly working just a few inches from the bottom of the lake. The most successful form of retrieve seems to be a long, slow, steady pull with the left hand and a lengthy pause between pulls. It will – as in any other type of wet-fly fishing – pay to experiment with differing types and speeds of retrieve. This is perhaps the most common fault with stillwater fly-anglers; they get into a rhythm of retrieve that suits *them* and they stick to it come hell or high water, *no matter what the fish wants, and also quite often without any thought of how the fly should be made to behave.* To expect a trout to take a nymph which is being retrieved at the same speed and in the same manner as a lure or an attractor-type wet fly is ridiculous; all it really takes is just a little thought and if that thought is applied correctly the number and size of fish taken by the angler from any given water will quite easily be doubled or trebled over a season.

The straightforward mechanics of casting are most certainly the easiest thing to learn with regard to fly-fishing; the harder parts come with the learning of the more detailed but far more important aspects of the use of the correct pattern and its application to the fishing of that day. Another thing that most people do not seem to realise is that conditions alter very considerably from day to day. On two identical-*seeming* days a complete alteration in the underwater feeding pattern of the fish can have been effected by something like a drop in water temperature of a degree or so, just because the cloudcover dispersed for three or four hours in the middle of the night whereas the night before the clouds held in the heat. Almost invariably, though, the angler goes out and uses the same techniques and methods he used the day before with some success and wonders why they fail on the following day. If a little thought and imagination had been employed the results might have been far more satisfying. A positive approach to fishing is most important, it is not really much good going out, looking at the water and thinking that conditions look hopeless and therefore fishing in a desultory manner. Look at the conditions of the day and try to imagine *where you* would be and on *what you* might be feeding were you a fish; it will not always work by any means but if you get into the habit of doing this, a store of knowledge – often subconscious knowledge– is called into play, and over a long period you will find that you are more and more correct in your 'guesswork'. It is *always* far better to look at the fishing and the fish with a positive attitude rather than being negative about them.

I do not quite know how I was side-tracked into telling you those stories; anyway we shall now get on with the Muddler. Most keen reservoir fly-fishermen have at least a couple of these flies in their box these days but many people who tie their own flies have had a problem – this is, correctly applying that 'head' of deer hair to the front of the fly. It is this that gives this fly its unique appearance, and although people have tried other methods of applying it there is only one way that I find completely satisfactory. (Just look at that, I am being dogmatic again – as sure as fate someone will now come up with a better method!) It is really quite easy to do, and the results are very gratifying, both in terms of the finished fly and with regard to the fish it catches.

Method of tying

The first thing to do with this pattern is to dress the rear portion of the fly; tail, body and wings. Start the tying silk about *one-third of the way down the shank from the eye,* leave the front third clear of silk. Wind the silk down the shank to the bend and tie in two strips of either oak turkey tail or wing feather as a tail. The straight-tail effect that I explained when writing of the Butcher patterns is again needed here. Carry the silk up the body, binding down the surplus part of the tail as you go to secure the tail really firmly and to make the body as smooth and even as possible. Do not take the silk past the point where it was first tied in; you will want that piece of bare hook shank later to take the ruff and the head.

Next tie in a strip of gold Lurex or tinsel, take it down to the tail in close-butted turns and then come back up the body and tie in and trim off where it was first fixed. Now take two strips of the same material you used for the tail and tie in the wings. Make these strips about twice as wide as the tail strips.

Now for what most people consider the tricky bit. Cut off a

Muddler Minnow

fair sized bunch of deer *body hair* – it must be body hair, buck-tail for instance is not thick enough. Hold this bunch in your left hand with the stubs pointing out over the hook eye, take two *very loose* turns of silk over the hair and round the bare shank, release the hair and at the same time pull the silk taut. The hair will flare out round the shank of the hook. With your left hand gently compress the fibres as much as possible and take two or three tight turns of silk round the shank in front of the hair to hold it firmly in place. Keep repeating this operation until the front of the hook is filled with the splayed-out hair. Secure all with a good whip finish, *do not* as yet varnish the head.

You have now come to the part where a vacuum cleaner is almost an essential unless you happen to have a very, very understanding wife! Take your scissors and trim the head to shape. I like a round, ball-shaped head generally. Others prefer a cylindrical shape or a cone tapering towards the eye. It will pay you to tie up the various types and see which shape catches more fish for you. When trimming off the ruff you should leave some of the fibres, the tapering ones, not the stubs, pointing back over the body. This is why the first bunch of hair is always tied in with the stubs pointing over the hook eye. Some fly-dressers like to add a hair-wing before the ruff is tied in, I usually find that the fibres from the ruff are sufficient, though. A coat or two of varnish finishes the job.

The Dressing (see Plate 7)

Silk: Brown (Sherry Spinner)
Tail: Oak turkey tail or wing
Body: Gold tinsel or Lurex
Wing: As for tail, with hair added if required
Ruff: Deer body hair
Head: As for Ruff
Hooks: 4 – 12 long shank, Old Numbers

WHISKEY MUDDLER

Albert Whillock tells me that this pattern has been doing as well if not better than the original, the Whiskey Fly, particularly at Hanningfield reservoir where this fly has accounted for more trout than any other fly over the last couple of seasons. I have tried this pattern myself on two different waters and each time it caught fish, quite big fish too. But I tied a 'variant' which incorporated Dick Walker's idea of the lead strip tied in along the top of the hook shank and the dressing reversed so that the wing comes under the fly. This means that it can be fished along the bottom with virtually no danger of snagging up, a similar idea to the Keel hook except that this method does not suffer from the problem of missed takes to anywhere near the same degree as that experienced with Keel hooks. I have also used this method for various lures with great success. The Ace of Spades is particularly good when dressed in this way. A lot of the bigger trout feed almost exclusively on the bottom and any fly or method which enables these fish to be caught is to be welcomed. These very large trout, usually browns, are of no real benefit to the fishery and some method of catching them has long been needed. I can see no very good reason why the various reservoirs should not open their waters to all methods of fishing for perhaps a week at the end of the season. Live or dead baits fished hard on the bottom would certainly catch these big trout where the fly-angler has very little chance. This would rid the waters of protein-consuming fish that contribute very little to the sporting aspect of the lakes; it would also have the additional benefit of raising the average weights considerably which would certainly help the reservoirs in their search for publicity...

Anyway, until we have water management committees sufficiently forward-looking to consider these or similar proposals we shall have to continue to search for fly-fishing methods and patterns which can perhaps help to contact these very large trout. The Walker method of leading the backs of flies and lures may well be a contributory factor in doing this; at least you can put the fly where it will do most good.

Method of tying
Exactly the same body is used for this pattern as is used for the Whiskey Fly, except that it is kept to the rear portion of the hook so that a fair length of hook is kept bare to receive the deer hair head and ruff. A wing of oak turkey is again tied in and over this

Whiskey Muddler

a small bunch of orange calf tail is secured. Make certain you use those locking turns I discussed in the chapter on Hair-wings. The head is then applied in the way described for the normal Muddler Minnow.

The Dressing (see Plate 8)

Silk:	Scarlet fluorescent floss
Tag:	As for silk
Body:	Gold or silver Sellotape, varnished
Rib:	As for silk
Wing:	Oak turkey and orange dyed calf tail
Ruff:	Deer body hair
Head:	As for ruff
Hooks:	6 – 8 long shank, Old Numbers

LESLIE'S LURE AND WALKER'S KILLER

I have included these two flies under the same heading because the dressings are rather similar, the basic principles and shapes being virtually the same.

When I first started stillwater fly-fishing I went though the book to find flies that would be effective fish-takers during different periods of the season. Leslie's Lure was one that came to my rescue on one particular day and in rather unusual circumstances. I remember standing up to my wader-tops casting as far as I could reach with no effect whatsoever – when one starts at any sport one tends to copy the approach used by other people – no trout was even vaguely interested in what I had to offer him. It was late April and nothing appeared to be moving on or under that leaden water. Fast becoming despondent (patience was never one of my major virtues!) I had just decided to return to the bank for a pull at my hip flask when I saw a very strange sight indeed: fish were moving close to the shore, six or eight feet from the bank the water was boiling ...

I had tramped, without thought and without knowing they were there, past a lot of busily feeding trout. And they were now feeding directly between the bank and myself! I was astounded, nobody had ever told me trout behaved in this strange way. It did teach me though that time and thought should be used before wading into the water.

Seeing these fish, I could not just turn around and tramp to the bank and start from scratch – that would really have frightened the life out of them. No, I had to fish from where I stood, I looked at the feeding orgy taking place and wondered just what could be causing it. There was no fly on the water and it was much too early for the coarse-fish fry. What then? Suddenly it dawned on me. Of course: tadpoles! I had noticed a few round my waders as I entered the water and it must have been these that were sending the trout wild. I frantically searched through my fly-box for something – anything – that looked even remotely

Walker's Killer

like an immature frog and saw, tucked away in a corner, a Leslie's Lure. I had never tried it before, but it *was* the right shape at least. I tied it on the leader and dabbled it through the water at my feet, it looked as if it might, just might, do the trick. On my second cast the fly sank to the bottom in about six inches of water and I slowly retrieved it, stop-and-start. A fish came at it with most of his back out of the water but he turned away at the last moment. After a couple more casts I found that what the trout wanted was a slow, steady retrieve. The takes were confident and the hook held in the scissors. Each time I hooked a trout I hustled it out into the deeper water to avoid disturbing the others. The fight those trout put up in that shallow water had to be seen to be believed. I remember that I took five before the others were scared off, that in a matter of half-an-hour.

Method of tying
Leslie's Lure is a New Zealand fly and fairly simple to dress. I would advise anybody fishing stillwater in the early season to carry a few; you never know when you are going to come across those tadpoling trout. Another fly which can be equally effective when the trout are doing this is Walker's Killer, a South African pattern. I have found that this fly will also take trout when fished on a sunk line over deep water; Leslie's Lure does not seem to work anywhere near as well in those circumstances – funny that . . .

Run the tying silk down to the hook bend and tie in quite a big bunch of squirrel tail hair as a tail, taking a couple of locking turns round the fibres really to secure them. Now catch in the ribbing tinsel and the end of the chenille, tie in just the central core of this material as you did for the Ace of Spades. Wind the chenille up the body to within about an eighth of an inch from the eye, tie in and trim off the spare end. The body is now ribbed neatly with the tinsel and the end tied in and trimmed off.

The wings are rather different from any I have discussed previously because they are tied in *alongside* the body, *not* on top of the hook as with most wet-fly patterns. In fact they completely shield the body from view. You will need four feathers for the wing, and they should be stripped of sufficient fibres so that when laid alongside the hook the tips just reach the bend. They are best if they are tied in in pairs, the inside pair just slightly shorter than the outside pair. This produces a streamlined appearance and avoids any ugly lumps at the head. Apply a good whip finish and put on two or three coats of varnish.

The materials for Walker's Killer (nothing whatever to do with Dick) are rather similar. You need a black cock's hackle – a spade hackle is best – red chenille, and eighteen, yes, that's right, eighteen! brown partridge hackles. I have found that in use the hackles with the pale stripe down the middle have done best for me.

A bunch of hackle fibres is tied in as a tail and the chenille is then wound up the body for about two-thirds of its length. The hackle feathers are tied in to make the wing in the same way as for the previous fly, but they are tied in as three layers of three feathers, gradually working towards the eye. Make a nice sleek head and varnish, and there you are: one of South Africa's most effective flies. May you do as well with it as I have.

The Dressings (see Plate 8)

	Leslie's Lure
Silk:	Black
Tail:	Brown barred squirrel tail
Rib:	Oval silver tinsel
Body:	Yellow, red or green chenille
Wing:	Hen pheasant wing feathers from the outside front edge
Hooks:	4 – 10, Old Numbers

	Walker's Killer
Silk:	Black or brown
Tail:	Black cock hackle
Body:	Red chenille
Wing:	18 partridge hackles
Hooks:	4 Old Numbers

WORMFLY

I have met anglers who seem to take the name of this fly literally and expect it to be an imitation of a brandling or a lobworm: it is not. Mind you, I would rather that nobody asked me just what it is supposed to imitate, because I cannot think of anything that looks remotely like a Wormfly – unless it is another Wormfly.

This is really quite a simple fly to dress, the reason why they are fairly expensive to purchase in the shops is that they are tied on tandem hooks. This means that you have to make up the same sort of mount you use for the multi-hook lures, and that takes time. All the Wormfly really consists of is two Red Tags tied in tandem. There is a tandem-hook rig available on the market at the moment and if this was satisfactory it would be just the thing for tying Wormflies or lures; the snag is that it is far from satisfactory. For a start the batch I tried were all as soft as putty and I could straighten them out in my fingers; heaven help you if you hooked a decent trout on them. The other snag is that the two hooks are not brazed together one behind the other but with one hook on top of the other. A very long-shanked hook with another fixed on top of it and not underneath as it should be; the *only* reason for this peculiar state of affairs according to a wholesaler I spoke to was because it was easier for the manufacturers to do them this way, the efficacy of the finished item apparently did not come into it. I should imagine that some manufacturer of good-quality hooks could make quite a nice little sum for himself if he was to do the job properly; it surely would not be so difficult to arrange. Just think of the problems it would cure: no fiddling about making up lure mounts, no weak link for a trout's teeth to fray, and it would make for a stronger and cheaper job generally. I for one should not mind in the slightest being charged three or even four times the cost of an ordinary hook if I could buy tandems made up in this way.

Method of tying

First of all make up a mount in exactly the same way you did for the Black Lure. When it is finished and the adhesive has dried, you run your tying silk down the length of the rear hook, at the bend you tie in a short tag of scarlet floss silk. Some people say they get better results by using a tag of scarlet or orange fluorescent wool. After the tag is tied in, a body of twisted peacock herl strands is wound up the shank – on any herl or feather fibre body

Wormfly

it is advisable to wind over a coating of wet varnish, it will make the finished fly much stronger. When you have tied in and trimmed off the ends of the body materials you wind a hackle of red cock at the front of the hook. As with all the wet-hackled patterns I spoke about earlier this hackle should be tied in at an angle so that the fibres slope back over the body slightly. Whip-finish the head and varnish it.

Exactly the same procedure is used for the front half of the fly. You can, if you wish, leave out the second tag; feelings seem to be slightly mixed about this, some of my customers prefer them tied with two tags but others (the majority) like them tied with just the tag on the rear hook. I frankly doubt that it makes much difference one way or the other.

The Dressing (see Plate 8)
Silk: Brown (Sherry Spinner)
Tags: Red floss, red or orange fluorescent wool
Bodies: Bronze peacock herl
Hackles: Red cock
Hooks: 8 – 14, two in tandem, Old Numbers

SALMON FLIES

CHAPTER SIXTEEN

LOW-WATER PATTERNS

BLUE CHARM

My opportunities for catching salmon are somewhat restricted – there is a noticeable shortage of salmon rivers in Surrey! When I do get the chance of a few days after them, I take it, those chances come along all too infrequently. A few years ago I went up to a river in mid-Wales; apparently I had timed it just about right because the afternoon I arrived it started to rain and rain and rain. . . . The river rose from its previous low, almost drought conditions and the fish began to run up it.

My enquiries at the local tackle-shop informed me that my only real chance of fish was on the ubiquitous worm. I had come up on the off-chance and the only tackle I had with me was my usual reservoir trouting outfit, not really suitable for worming, at least I did not think so. So I decided to try the fly. I must have been in a devil of a hurry to leave home because all the flies I had with me – all the salmon flies at any rate – were low-water patterns. I had left all the fully dressed patterns in my tackle-room. It was not a very auspicious start.

After prospecting the raging waters at my disposal I settled on a pool about fifty feet long at the bottom of a set of fearsome rapids. It looked like a spot where any sensible fish would want to rest up before the long hard climb ahead. After fishing the tail of the pool for a while without any real interest being shown in the fly (a Blue Charm) I moved upstream into the centre section. Immediately I had a hard take and a fish started roaring all over the pool. After about five minutes I had him fairly well beaten, and he slipped first time into the landing-net. A 7lb grilse, all silvery and glistening, and his tail section well covered with the sea-lice that showed he was a fresh-run fish. My very next cast to the same spot was taken again, this time a five-pounder.

215

After two more hours I had taken five fish from an ounce or two over five pounds to a beautiful nine and three-quarter pounder. I was exhausted. Indeed I was satiated with all these salmon wanting to give themselves up! I decided that five was plenty and settled down to have a snooze in a nearby barn. About four hours later I woke up and went back to my pool, not to fish but merely to look at it. Someone else was there, a shadowy figure on the rocks right at the top of the pool, partly hidden by a couple of spindly oak trees; he was fishing.

I thought that it would be pleasant to watch someone else at work and see how he did, so I took my sandwiches and flask and strolled up the bank. At my wishing him good afternoon he turned round with what I thought looked a bit like a guilty start and mumbled something in reply. He was an extraordinary old chap, about seventy-five to eighty, dressed in ragged jacket and trousers that looked as if they had once been Oxford bags; his tackle and method of using it were a marvel . . . The rod was a solid glass, 6ft long brute of a thing, like a poker and the sort of rod that was once used on piers up and down the country. The reel was a heavy-duty sea fixed-spool that had definitely seen better days. The line – well, that *really* was something, I reckoned the breaking strain to be between thirty and forty pounds and it had a multitude of knots throughout its length. Attached to this line was a lead that must have weighed half a pound, one of those round jobs with a hole in the middle and spiky bits on the rim. They are normally sold for use with sea hand-lines on a winder. His hook was about size 2/0 and impaled on this was a bunch of at least four lobworms.

His technique was simple, extremely effective and if somewhat crude it did have the merit of being straightforward! At his feet there was a tiny patch of nearly stationary water, right at the foot of the falls. The lead was dropped into this, the rod was then balanced on a rock, and our hero settled back and puffed at a particularly filthy-smelling pipe. I sat down a few yards back from the water and after offering him a cup of coffee – which was refused – I started to eat my sandwiches. As I looked up from the first bite I saw that 'rod' begin to describe an arc which must have taken it into the river, before I could call a warning a horny old hand shot out and grabbed the end of the butt. The rod was then pulled straight upwards and back over the old man's shoulder, a fish, a sewin, described a lovely arc and hit the ground behind him with a thump that I could feel from where I was sitting! Just like a cork out of a bottle that fish was – talk about the flying-fish technique! That sea trout must have weighed upwards of a pound and a half and the three or four fish that followed it were even heavier. It was fascinating to watch, and on each occasion the result was the same, the fish flying out of the water over his shoulder and thumping onto the ground. I thought it fairly obvious that he did not fish for sport . . . I also thought it equally obvious that small refinements like buying licences were not his style either, but it was an education and experience I would not have missed for the world. He departed as he had fished, silently, without a word and in a hurry; then I saw why. The bailiff had just turned the corner downstream of us and was coming up to check the licences. That old fellow knew his business all right; I should love to know just how many fish he extracted from that river by this method. I should also like to know what would happen if he connected with a large salmon, that must *really* be something to watch.

Since that day the Blue Charm has always had a special place in my fly-box and I cannot use it without remembering that pool, those five lovely grilse and an old figure sitting hunched over in the rain.

Method of tying

Taking salmon by what has become known as the 'greased-line' method has not had a long history. Now that the floating plastic-coated lines are used almost exclusively the name is perhaps an anomaly, but the basic idea and the method of use are the same. A lightly dressed fly is fished just below the surface on lightish tackle during low-water conditions. This technique has saved many an angler a blank when conditions dictated the use of this method. The basic theme of the low-water salmon fly is that the dressing should be as sparse as possible and only cover the front half or two-thirds of the light-wire hook shank.

Tie in black tying silk at the eye and carry it to about halfway

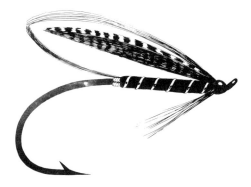

Blue Charm

down the shank, bind down the spurred eye very carefully with close-butted turns of silk as you go. Catch in a piece of round silver tinsel where the silk ends and wind four or five close, touching turns back towards the eye. Tie in and trim off the end. Build up a short length of tying silk in front of the tag until it is absolutely level with the turns of tinsel. Now tie in a tail of golden pheasant crest on top of the layers of silk, making certain it has a nice upwards curve to it and that it sits square on the hook; I like my low-water fly tails to reach just to the bend of the hook but many people tie them in shorter than that.

Oval silver tinsel for the rib is now tied in immediately in front of the tail and the silk is wound forward to within an eighth of an inch from the eye. Tie in a length of fine black floss, half of the twisted two-ply type. Wind it down to the tail and back up again to the eye, keeping the body as slim as you can. Rib the black body with even turns of the oval silver tinsel, tie in and trim off the end.

Reverse the hook in the vice and tie in a false or beard hackle of bright blue cock hackles. Do not make this hackle too heavy and remember to 'spread' it round the hook shank. Turn the hook the right way up again and make the wing using the folded-strip method I described in the section on wet flies. Over the lower bronze mallard wing tie in a thin piece of folded barred teal feather. It should be no more than a quarter of the depth of the mallard.

Finally, the topping of golden pheasant crest is tied in. Make certain you measure it against the fly so that when it is finally fixed the tips of the tail and the topping just meet. This is a difficult feather to tie in but I find it is a help if I hold the crest on a board and bring the blunt edge of a knife down on the exact spot where the fixing will go. This scores and flattens the stalk, it also bends it at this point. This makes the tying in much simpler.

Finish the head smoothly with the silk, whip-finish and varnish the head with enough coats to ensure that it comes up smooth and shiny.

The Dressing (see Plate 8)

Silk: Black
Tag: Round silver tinsel
Tail: Golden pheasant crest
Rib: Oval silver tinsel
Body: Black floss silk
Throat: Dyed blue cock hackle
Wing: Bronze mallard with teal strip over, topping over all
Head: Black varnish
Hooks: 1 – 12, low water, Old Numbers

WHITE DOCTOR

This is a fly which has never caught a salmon for me (not that that means much in itself – very few flies have!) but I have had some marvellous fun with sea trout on it, particularly down on the West Country rivers. I remember on one occasion I had been booked into a beat that looked absolutely hopeless; it was just one long glide with not a pool in it – in fact it had virtually no major features at all. It was merely smooth, unruffled water; at no point that I could see was it more than a foot or eighteen inches deep but in the three days I fished it I caught no less than fourteen good sea trout with the best fish going 1oz over 6lbs. When I first saw the water I quite thought that I should have to settle for catching the small brown trout on a dry fly; luckily, however, I saw a small salmon show on the far side of the water and I decided to try a low-water fly for him. No, I did not catch him but after an hour or so I did get a good take from a 3lb plus sea trout and that fired my enthusiasm for this uninteresting

White Doctor

looking stretch of water. The thing that did surprise me was that the far more attractive-looking pools both upstream and down failed to produce any fish of note over those three days.

Method of tying

All low-water salmon flies should be tied on the right type of hook, this needs, to be a strong, light-wire 'iron' which is sold specifically for this purpose. It can quickly lead to disaster if you try using the normal long-shank trout hooks, they just are not strong enough. If you are fishing a trout water where the fish run very big, and you are worried about hook breakages it can sometimes pay to use the low-water hooks for your trout fishing; they are expensive but it is well worth paying a little extra to ensure that once a fish is hooked it stays hooked. I can never imagine why so little attention is paid by anglers to their hooks; without doubt they are the most important single item in their tackle yet where a man will happily spend forty or fifty pounds buying the very best rod, reel and line, he will begrudge a couple of pence on a good quality hook.

All salmon irons should have a 'spur' of metal on them from which the eye is formed. The spur runs along the shank of the hook for about a quarter of its length. It is most important that this spur should be bound tight into the main shank with close-wound turns of silk. The main idea behind it is that it should not be possible for a hard-fighting salmon to open up the eye of the hook, as can sometimes happen with ring-eyes. It also means that the surface of the eye is perfectly smooth and there is no danger of the nylon leader being cut on a ragged edge.

After winding those close turns of silk over the spur, carry the silk down the shank for about half its length. Tie in a length of oval silver tinsel and wind a short tag, tie in and trim off the end. Immediately in front of this tag wind another one of yellow floss silk. Both these tags should be fairly short. Build up the turns of tying silk directly in front of the tag so that it lies perfectly level with the floss and then tie in the tail of golden pheasant crest feather. In front of the tail you wind a butt of scarlet wool. Some people like to tie in the wool as a strand but I much prefer to dub it onto the silk and then wind it on; this is because if it is tied as a strand it tends to pull apart under the slightest pressure and it does not wind in neatly. I think you will find you get much better results if you dub it on.

When the butt is finished – again do not make it too long, keep the proportions of the fly correct and remember that the fly is to be as lightly dressed as possible – tie in a length of oval silver tinsel for the rib. Run the tying silk back up the shank to slightly short of the eye and catch in a piece of white floss silk; wind this thinly down the body to meet the butt and then come back up the hook over the first layer to the eye, tie in and trim. Rib with the tinsel, making the ribbing evenly spaced, about five turns on a size 8 hook.

Reverse the fly in the vice and tie in a false hackle of pale blue cock and in front of this a few strands of blue jay hackle; turn the fly up the right way again in the vice. The wings are married strands on this fly; use exactly the same principle as that for the Parmachene Belle in the section on wet flies. Marry up the feathers in the order given in the dressing – all married wings start at the bottom. For example, if a dressing lists, as this one does, yellow, red, blue and green swan or goose with golden pheasant tail, they are tied in in that order with the yellow strip at the bottom of the wing. Match up the two wing sections so that they are perfectly level and tie them in as you would any other wing. The wing should reach not quite to the end of the tail feather.

On either side of the wing tie in one of the bright blue feathers taken from a kingfisher's rump. These are the very short feathers with the brightest colour, the duller feathers are nowhere near as good. You will have to strip off the fluff at the base of the kingfisher feather before you tie it in. Most dressers tie the sides in last but I always think that the most difficult part of the wing is the topping so I prefer to make things easy for myself and tie that in last of all. If this is not done it is only too easy for the topping to be forced to one side by the turns of tying silk when fixing in the kingfisher or the jungle cock which is needed on most salmon flies. It makes no difference to the finished appearance of the fly – unless, that is, it makes for a neater dressing. Treat the golden pheasant topping feather in exactly the same way you did for the Blue Charm and tie it in so that the very tips of the tail and the topping meet. If you have any difficulty with this feather as regards its shape, all you have to do is to wet it and then lay it on a piece of glass, stroke it to the correct shape and then gently press it into place. Leave it to dry and after an hour or so it will 'set' and retain the shape and curve you have given it. The window above my fly-dressing bench is a mass of little curved marks on the glass where I have stuck golden pheasant crests to it! Finish the head neatly and apply varnish until it is smooth as glass. A tip here; if you run a coat of fairly thick black varnish onto the head first and then put on a coat or two of clear over the top, it will be much quicker than just building up coats of clear on their own. The main thing, though, is to make sure that the turns of silk lie smoothly on the head before varnishing, that is half the battle.

The Dressing (see Plate 8)

Silk:	Black
Tag:	Silver tinsel and yellow floss
Tail:	Golden pheasant crest
Butt:	Scarlet wool
Rib:	Oval silver tinsel
Body:	White floss silk
Hackle:	Pale blue hackle with jay in front
Wings:	Married strands of yellow, red, blue and green swan or goose, golden pheasant tail

Sides: Blue kingfisher rump feather
Topping: Golden pheasant crest
Head: Black varnish
Hooks: 1 – 12, low-water, Old Numbers

THUNDER AND LIGHTNING

Along with the Blue Charm this fly is perhaps the most popular of the low-water flies. I have found it to be at its most effective in the evenings, mainly at the tail-end of pools. I like where possible to work it as slowly as I can across the current; the thrill that I get from seeing a large fish head and tail over it is perhaps the greatest that I get from any of my fishing. I like the Blue Charm or the White Doctor when the light is on the water, but as soon as evening approaches I seem to do much better with this pattern. The same thing applies with water which is coming down stained deep brown with peat, the Thunder and Lightning comes into its own then as well. I suppose it is the same basic principle which seems to apply to stillwater trouting, in bright conditions give them a bright fly so that the sun can reflect off the shiny or light-coloured surfaces but in dull or dark conditions they seem to prefer a fly with a darker silhouette. This does not apply to all flies; for instance the Ace of Spades which is purposely dressed to be as dark and dense as possible does very well during the day, but for most general purposes it is not a bad rule to follow.

Method of tying
Wind your tying silk down the shank of the hook as for the previous flies; it only wants to go down about half of its length. Catch in a strand of round gold tinsel and wind a short tag, and in front of this wind on another tag of yellow floss. Tie in a tail of golden pheasant crest and at the same point tie in the ribbing tinsel, oval gold. Wind the silk back up the shank over the ends of the tail and the ribbing material to secure them firmly, and just behind the eye tie in a length of black floss silk. Wind the floss down the body to butt up tight to the tail and then take it back to the point at which it was first tied in, trim off the end. Rib the body with evenly spaced turns of tinsel, tie in and trim.
Reverse the hook and fix in a beard hackle of orange cock fibres,

Thunder and Lightning

and in front of this tie in a few strands of jay hackle. Turn the fly the right way up again in the vice. I find it best to make the wing up from two wide strips of bronze mallard laid one on top of the other and then folded in half and tied in, it makes the silhouette sharper and the fly more dense. After the jungle cock is firmly secured alongside the wing you can then tie in the topping of golden pheasant crest. Tie it in in the same manner as that used for the other two low-water patterns. Finish the head neatly and apply varnish to it.

The Dressing (see Plate 8)

Silk:	Black
Tag:	Round gold tinsel and yellow floss
Tail:	Golden pheasant crest
Rib:	Oval gold tinsel
Body:	Black floss silk
Hackle:	Orange cock hackle with jay in front
Wings:	Bronze mallard
Sides:	Jungle cock
Topping:	Golden pheasant crest
Head:	Black varnish
Hooks:	1 – 12, low-water, Old Numbers

CHAPTER SEVENTEEN

FULLY DRESSED FLIES

JOCK SCOTT

One of the most prominent angling writers in the United Kingdom said that he considered the traditional salmon fly patterns as 'mere folklore'. I was saddened to read this for three reasons: – firstly, these flies have an ability to catch fish which has been proved over the years, many of them are far more effective than their more modern counterparts. Secondly, it could – because of this writer's influence and following – be discouraging to anyone thinking of using these flies for the first time and, finally, because the *art* (and I stress that word) of tying a really good salmon fly seems to be fast becoming a thing of the past.

Yes, these flies are complicated; it can take up to half an hour to tie just one, but a salmon fly really well tied by an expert will bring a sparkle to any angler's eye; they are indeed a work of art. They also, of course, take fish, which I suppose is the object of tying them in the first place. I like the traditional things in this life, and this is never more true than in tackle and things concerned with angling. I am not suggesting that we bring back lancewood tops to our rods, by the way! But I am saying that there is no reason to discard items of tackle that have proved their worth over the years. These should be preserved and used by future generations of anglers for whom they will work just as effectively as they did for their great-grandfathers. Salmon flies are well worth saving from the technological scrap-heap.

The Jock Scott is perhaps the most complicated of all the fully dressed patterns; a test for your fly-dressing skill if ever there was one. It is, I should think, a name that most anglers have heard, along with Greenwell's Glory, the Butcher, Durham Ranger and Wickham's Fancy: one of the *famous* names, one, that, I hope, will ne'er be forgot.

225

Jock Scott (Salmon)

Method of tying

Fasten your tying silk in at the eye and wind it down the shank to the bend, make certain that the turns of silk are tight and close over the 'spur', wind it to a point just short of the bend of the hook. The silk is wound as far as this only so that when the tail is tied in it will not protrude beyond the bend. There are other styles of dressing these flies that do take the tail well out beyond the bend of the hook but when I tried them I found that there were far more 'short takes' than if the whole fly were confined to just the hook length. Fine, round silver tinsel is now tied in and a tag is wound by first taking it down the shank towards the bend for four or five turns and then coming back up over the first layer and securing it. Make the turns tight, even and close-butted. A tail comprising a golden pheasant crest and an Indian crow feather is now tied in; first the crest and then on top of it the Indian crow or substitute. Make certain that they are set square on the top of the hook or the finished appearance of the fly will be spoiled.

A butt of black ostrich herl is now wound on so that it covers the stubs of the tail feathers; the flue on the stalk should face back towards the tail so that when it is wound on it makes a dense 'bush' with no sign of the stalk showing between turns. Now tie in a piece of oval silver tinsel (fine) to rib the back half of the body which is of golden yellow floss tied in about halfway up the shank and then wound down the hook to the butt and wound up the shank again over the first layer. The next operation is to apply the veiling. The standard dressing involves six or more toucan feathers but I have found that a far better job can be made of it by using golden pheasant body feathers (yellow gold), these being tied in with about three turns of silk and then gently pulled through until the tips just reach the front edge of the butt. Four are usually enough. The next thing is to wind another butt, just like the one at the tail but this time covering up the ends of the veiling material. Heavy oval silver tinsel is now tied in to rib the front half of the body which is made of black floss silk. A black cock hackle is tied in at the head and wound palmer-fashion down the body to the forward butt and secured by the ribbing tinsel which is wound on the opposite spiral; make certain that both ribs go up the body the same way. I have been criticised because I prefer to use a hackle from which one side of the fibres has been stripped rather than the more usual doubled hackle; I like it much better this way because it makes the hackle sparser, gives more life and action to it in the water and also ensures that *all* the fibres slope backwards. This is virtually impossible to achieve by the practice of doubling. Certainly – in my opinion at any rate – it makes for better-looking fly and a better fish-taker.

Reverse the fly in the vice so that a throat hackle of speckled guinea fowl can be tied in as a beard. Do not make the fibres too long; they should just about reach the tail butt and do not forget to spread them so that they fan out and soften the outline of the fly. Turn the fly back up the right way again and tie in two strips of web taken from a white-tipped black turkey tail feather. These form the base of the built wing which is to follow.

Now to the part of the salmon flies which is generally considered to be the most difficult. It is not really, you know, not if it is done correctly. You have got to marry the strips of winging material together in exactly the same way that I described for the trout version of this fly in the wet-fly section. When the wing is made you take the two sections, match the tips so that they are perfectly level and then gently grasp the top edge of the wing. The bottom will flare open and you can lower the two pieces into place over the turkey tail strips; do not obscure them completely. Tie in the married wing in the normal way. The wing will now look extremely bright but by the time it is finished it will have been dulled by being overlaid by other materials.

Over the top of the wing tie in two strands taken from a peacock sword feather. These are tied in to lie flat over the wing and in my opinion this is by far the most difficult part of the dressing; a nasty intransigent feather this is, it always wants to splay out at weird angles. It takes perseverance to make it sit correctly over the wing. (Maybe this is why so many fly-dressers leave it out of the dressing!) Narrow strands of teal and barred summer duck or mandarin duck are married and then tied in to lie along the side of the wing. *Thin* strips of brown mallard are tied in so that they enclose the entire top portion of the wing. Once again the folded strip method does this best. Normally at this point you would tie in a golden pheasant crest to go right over the top of the fly and form a smooth curve that meets up with the tail crest; you can do this if you wish but I prefer to put on the topping last of all.

Along the side of the wing you now have to tie in a pair of jungle cock eye feathers. These should extend for slightly over half the length of the wing; remember, do not tear off the fibres at the base of the feathers, trim them with scissors. Squeeze the feather gently into the wing and pull it through three or four turns of silk so that it lies tight up to the side of the wing. The next feathers to go on the wing are two cheek feathers of either blue chatterer (which is now unobtainable) or kingfisher rump feathers. Finally I put on the topping of golden pheasant crest. You should try to avoid making the heads on your salmon flies too long; a short, stumpy head is the thing to aim for. Put on a coat of black varnish and follow this with several coats of clear until you have got a smooth, glossy head.

The Dressing (see Plate 8)

Silk:	Black
Tag:	Round silver tinsel
Tail:	Golden pheasant-crest and Indian crow
Butt:	Black dyed ostrich herl

Ribs:	Fine oval silver over rear half of fly, broader oval silver over the front half.
Body:	In two equal halves. First half golden yellow floss, veiled with golden pheasant rump feather or toucan. Butted with black ostrich herl. Front half black floss.
Hackle:	Black cock over black floss
Throat:	Speckled guinea fowl
Wings:	A pair of white-tipped black turkey tail strips (back to back). Over these, but not completely covering them: a mixed sheath of 'married strands' of (working from the bottom up) peacock wing, yellow, scarlet and blue swan or goose, bustard, florican bustard and golden pheasant tail. Two strands of peacock sword feather over. Barred summer duck or mandarin duck married to strips of teal on the sides. Brown mallard over.
Sides:	Jungle cock
Cheeks:	Blue kingfisher
Topping:	Golden pheasant crest
Head:	Black varnish
Hooks:	7/0 – 10, Old Numbers

DURHAM RANGER

This pattern is another of the famous names in fishing; it is also an extremely useful fly to have in one's box. I usually carry at least seven or eight in different sizes – I must say, though, that when it has proved successful for me it has been in the larger sizes, from 2 to 1/0. The Durham Ranger is classified as a 'whole-feather winged fly', this as opposed to the Jock Scott which is a built winged fly, the Thunder and Lightning which is classed as a strip-winged pattern or the Silver Wilkinson which is a mixed-wing fly. There are of course several others such as the Spey patterns, the grubs and prawns, tube flies and hair-wing patterns and even a few dry flies; in my opinion the latter are largely a waste of time from the fishing point of view. They do very occasionally take salmon but in the conditions that allow for their use I think you will find that far more fish will succumb to the low-water flies I wrote about earlier.

Method of tying

Run tying silk down the shank of the iron from the eye to slightly in front of the bend, tie in and wind a tag of round silver tinsel at this point. Build up the tying silk behind the tag so that when the tail is tied in it will lie true and not be twisted out of shape. The tail consists of a golden pheasant crest with Indian crow or its substitute over the top, the same as the Jock Scott in fact. In front of the tail wind on a butt of black ostrich herl.

The ribs are the next items to be tied in, these consist of silver twist (oval silver tinsel will do at a pinch but the finished item will not have the same appearance as it would have if twist were used), flat silver tinsel or Lurex and again silver twist. Three ribs in all. Tie them in in that order. There are four sections to the body and they are fairly important, or at least the colours are. The sections should be equal in length, and the first is of lemon floss silk, in front of this orange seal's fur is dubbed on – some people prefer to use wool and wind it in as a strand, but I think this spoils this fly – and then two more sections of seal's fur in fiery brown and black; stop the black so that there is enough room at the eye to tie in the wing.

The hackle for this pattern is a badger hackle dyed yellow. Without doubt if you are tying only a few of these flies for your own use it is a waste of expensive hackles to dye the whole cape. This is where the marker pens again come into their own. Buy a

Durham Ranger

yellow one and press the fibre end against a hard surface onto the hackle to be dyed, start at the butt end of the feather and then pull it through firmly in one movement, I usually do the 'bad' side of the hackle first and then turn it over and apply the marker pen again to the shiny side. This will leave you with a splendidly dyed feather without having committed a whole cape to dyeing. It really is very fast and easy, and the finish is extremely professional. As I have stated previously, I much prefer to strip the fibres off one side of my salmon fly body hackles as opposed to doubling them, this I now do and tie in the butt of the hackle at the eye and, taking the hackle pliers and clipping them on the tip of the hackle, wind it palmer-fashion down the body to the butt.

Now we come to what I consider to be the critical part of the Durham Ranger's dressing, the ribbing. First of all I wind the forward piece of twist up the body binding down the stalk of the hackle en route. This rib is tied in and trimmed off at the eye. I then pick out with the dubbing needle any fibres of hackle that may have been crushed out of place and then very carefully indeed I wind the flat silver tinsel rib up the body following the exact line taken by the first piece of twist. These two ribs are close-butted; there should be none of the body material showing through. When the flat rib is tied in and trimmed off I run the final rib up the body on the other side of the flat tinsel. The finished effect is of the flat rib enclosed by two touching outside ribs of twist; it takes a lot of practice to get everything absolutely correct but once it is achieved I am certain you will be delighted with the result. The centre rib should be judged for width according to the size of the finished fly, for example, from sizes 10 to 2 I would use the 1/64th of an inch width of Lurex and on the bigger sizes I would use the 1/32nd of an inch width.

The fly is turned over in the vice and a throat hackle of light blue cock is tied in. Turn the fly right way up again in the vice. A pair of jungle cock feathers are now tied in, these need to be fairly long and to reach almost to the tail crest feather. On either side of these a pair of tippet feathers are tied in so that they reach nearly three-quarters of the jungle cock's length, four tippet feathers in all. These *have* to be tied in together, otherwise they will force the wing to the side because the stalks are so strong.

Nothing but a muddle will result from trying to tie in first one side and then the other; believe me, I speak from experience!

On the outside of the wing a pair of jungle cock feathers are tied in which should reach just about half the length of the wing. Tie them in in the normal way. Cheeks of blue kingfisher rump are tied in on the outside of the jungle cock. A pair of horns of blue and yellow macaw tail feather are now tied in so that they come either side of the wing; just two strands are used. The final job I do – as always – is to apply the topping of golden pheasant crest. A final tip at this point: it greatly helps the appearance of the finished fly if the topping and the tail crest are doubled, in other words tie in two crest feathers for the tail and two for the topping. This does not seem to work very well on most salmon flies but I have found that it makes the Durham Ranger more attractive to both fish and man.

The Dressing (see Plate 8)

Silk:	Black
Tag:	Round silver tinsel
Tail:	Golden pheasant crest and Indian crow or substitute
Butt:	Black ostrich herl
Ribs:	Silver twist, flat silver tinsel or Lurex and silver twist
Body:	In quarters, lemon floss silk, orange, fiery brown and black seal's fur
Hackle:	Yellow dyed badger hackle
Throat:	Light blue cock's hackle
Wings:	A pair of jungle cock feathers, back to back. Outside these, two pairs of tippet feathers
Sides:	Jungle cock feathers
Cheeks:	Blue kingfisher rump
Horns:	Two strands of blue and yellow macaw tail
Topping:	Golden pheasant crest
Head:	Black varnish
Hooks:	5/0 – 10, salmon irons

MAR LODGE

The basic shading of this pattern is fairly light in tone, and I have found it does best when used in fairly bright conditions. I also use a simplified version tied as a low-water fly and it has proved its worth when there is little water coming down the river.

Method of tying

Bind down the spur of the loop eye on the iron with close-butted turns of silk and then run the silk down the shank to a position just before the bend of the hook. Tie in a tag of round silver tinsel and after building up a layer of tying silk to the same level as the tag, tie in the tail. This consists of a golden pheasant crest and a pair of small jungle cock feathers tied in 'back to back' on top of it. It is not at all easy to get the jungle cock feathers to sit correctly but I have found the best way of doing it is to cut off the fibres at the base of the feathers – as I have suggested previously – trim the two feathers to the length required and then *tear* off a fair portion of the remaining under-fibres so that when they are tied in as a tail they will be able to sit lower on the hook.

In front of the tail wind a butt of black ostrich herl – on this fly I like the butt to be shorter than on most salmon flies. Even on the larger sizes I rarely use more than three or four turns. Next tie in a length of oval silver tinsel. Wind the tying silk up the shank for a third of its length and tie in a piece of embossed silver tinsel. I prefer to use the very narrow material; run this down the shank to meet the butt and then come back up the body over the first layer and tie off where the fixing was made. Run the silk up the shank again for another third of its length and repeat the above operation with black floss silk. The final third is

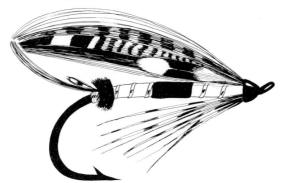

Mar Lodge

treated in exactly the same way as the first. Wind a neat, evenly spaced rib up the body and tie off and trim just behind the eye.

The fly is now turned upside down in the vice so that a hackle of guinea fowl can be tied in. Make this fairly full without being over-bulky, there is no body hackle on this pattern. Turn the fly right way up again to receive the wing.

This is an extremely difficult wing to marry up. It incorporates materials such as barred summer duck feather which is soft in texture but it also has strips of turkey tail and golden pheasant tail which are the reverse, and it is no easy matter to get the two joined. When it is successful the result is a most attractive-looking wing, and well worth the effort. Marry up strands of the feathers listed in the dressing with the yellow swan at the bottom, match up the two wing sections and then tie in in the normal way. At the sides of the wing secure two jungle cock feathers. I prefer these to be tied in slightly shorter than on most of the salmon patterns; certainly they should not reach for more than half of the wing's length. The next thing is the golden pheasant crest required as a topping: make certain the tips of this feather and the tips of the tail meet exactly. Wind a neat small head and make a good whip finish, then put on several coats of varnish.

The Dressing (see Plate 8)

Silk:	Black
Tag:	Round silver tinsel
Tail:	Golden pheasant crest with jungle cock over
Butt:	Black ostrich herl
Rib:	Oval silver tinsel
Body:	In thirds, silver embossed tinsel (flat), black floss and then embossed tinsel again
Hackle:	Speckled guinea fowl
Wing:	Yellow, red and blue swan or goose, peacock wing, barred summer duck or mandarin duck, grey mallard, dark speckled turkey wing, golden pheasant tail
Sides:	Jungle cock
Topping:	Golden pheasant crest
Head:	Black varnish
Hooks:	3/0 – 10, salmon irons

BLUE DOCTOR

Like the Mar Lodge this fly is classed as a 'mixed-wing' pattern and is invariably worth trying if the fish seem to be 'coming short', I do not know if it is the scarlet head that makes the fish take more firmly but something certainly seems to affect their response to this fly. The head is normally made of scarlet wool – as is the butt – several people have told me that when these are made of scarlet fluorescent wool the fish seem even keener. I have not tried this yet but it seems a reasonable assumption that if it is the head that causes the salmon to take further up the hook then fluorescent material would make this even more pronounced. Perhaps if DRF nylon floss were used it would be possible to varnish over it as is done in the Whiskey Fly, and this would make for a much firmer fixing. I often use this fly with a scarlet varnished head which seems to achieve the same results as the wool while remaining securely attached to the hook, unlike the wool. If you do decide to use wool then I would advise winding this over wet varnish as it is tied in, this will certainly help a little.

Method of tying
Wind the silk down the shank in the normal manner until you reach a point just short of the bend, there you catch in a piece of round silver tinsel and wind a short tag, in front of this wind another tag of golden yellow floss silk. Build up the turns of tying silk directly in front of the tag and tie in a tail consisting of a

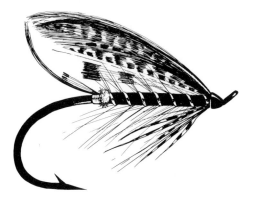

Blue Doctor

golden pheasant crest and a few fibres of golden pheasant tippet. The butt, which is made of scarlet wool, is normally wound on as a strand but I prefer to dub it, as it is far easier to get a smooth, even finish with dubbing.

Directly in front of the butt tie a piece of oval silver tinsel in, which is of a gauge appropriate to the size of the hook being used. Run the tying silk up the shank to the eye and catch in a length of light blue floss silk. Wind this in the normal manner down the shank to meet the butt and then come back up over the first layer to the eye again, tie in and trim off the surplus.

The body hackle should be chosen so that it matches the colour of the body material as nearly as possible. The hackle is tied in by the butt and wound down the shank to meet the rib which is taken up the body, through the hackle on the opposite spiral so that the tinsel secures the whole of the hackle throughout its length. Many people say the ribs on salmon flies should be made to follow the hackle stalk up the shank and lie alongside it; certainly this makes for a prettier fly which will look grand in a frame when it is on display. Unhappily, the fly tied in this fashion does not last very long when it is being fished; the hackle stalk, particularly at its tip, is a fragile thing, very easily broken. For practical angling purposes it is far better to wind the rib through the hackle and make certain the hackle stays intact.

Turn the fly over in the vice and tie in a throat hackle of blue jay wing feather. It will be found that while the jay feather is fine on the smaller sizes of fly it just is not long enough for flies tied on 1/0 hooks or bigger. The best substitute is blue gallena or blue dyed guinea fowl.

Put the fly the correct way up in the vice again and tie in the basic wing which consists of strands of golden pheasant tippet with strips of golden pheasant tail tied in over the top, much like a 'roof wing'. The best way to tie in the tippet fibres is to choose a large feather from the base of the cape, tear off the fluffy fibres at the butt end until you reach the clearly marked part of the feather. Now you tear or cut off two strips of equal width, lay them back to back and then tie them in. A neater finish will be obtained if this method is used rather than tearing off just one strip from one side of the feather. When the roof of golden pheasant tail is tied in, the next job is to marry up strands of feather in the normal way and in the order given in the dressing and tie these in over the top of the basic wing; do not hide the underwing completely with the married strands.

Marry up strips taken from either barred summer duck feathers or mandarin duck feathers and narrow strips of teal. Tie these in on either side of the wing, to make them lie flat against the wing. Take two or three turns of silk over the butts of the feathers and then gently pull them through the silk until the strips are the correct length, trim off the ends. Tie in a narrow roof wing of folded strips of brown mallard feather over the top of the wing. Now the topping of golden pheasant crest is tied in to complete the winging. This pattern is one of the few salmon flies that do not have jungle cock sides. Many people like to tie in cheeks of blue kingfisher rump feather, and I must say that I prefer the fly tied in this way. Now either dub in or wind on a head of scarlet wool (or fluorescent material if you wish). Do not forget that if you use wool you must wind it on over wet varnish. Make a neat whip finish right at the tip of the eye and run over two or three coats of clear varnish.

The Dressing (see Plate 8)

Silk: Black or scarlet
Tag: Round silver tinsel and golden floss
Tail: A golden pheasant crest and a few strands of tippet
Butt: Scarlet wool
Rib: Oval silver tinsel
Body: Light blue floss silk
Hackle: Cock hackle to match body material
Throat: Blue jay or blue gallena
Wings: Golden pheasant tippet in strands roofed with golden pheasant tail strips. Married strips of dyed swan or goose, scarlet, blue and yellow, florican bustard, peacock wing, oak turkey tail. Married strips of barred summer duck or mandarin duck and teal breast feather. A roof of narrow strips of bronze mallard feather.
Cheeks: Blue kingfisher

Topping: Golden pheasant crest

Head: Scarlet wool, red varnish, or scarlet fluorescent wool or floss

Hooks: 3/0 – 10, salmon irons

COLLYER'S BLUE

The room where I dress flies is known as the 'Inner Sanctum' to all and sundry, and the privilege and honour of being invited to enter that awful shambles is something accorded to very few. Of those few one was my best retail customer; unhappily he is now dead, but what an angler he was. A retired sea captain, he had fished in virtually every country in the world that has a coastline. His tales of blue marlin, bonefish and tiger fish would stir the soul of any angler, but his real love was the Atlantic salmon. How he did love those fish...

One day he came up to watch me dressing some low-water patterns for him (he had an invitation to fish an exclusive river in Scotland that weekend and was in his usual panic). When this kind of thing happened he became very authoritarian and nobody could have dreamt of defying him. By hook or by crook he would have those Blue Charms. About a week before his visit I had been messing about (as I am always doing), tying up and experimenting with different patterns, which almost invariably are consigned to the rubbish pile – that is one corner of the room which I rarely use and which is cleared up about once a year – and one of these experimental flies caught his eye and he felt suddenly that this was *it*. He had to have some, right now, of course, in time for his trip. I protested in vain that it was a fly that was only a rough and that I had not even dreamed up a name for it, it was quite untested, and so on. He would have none of it, 'I want 'em', he bellowed, 'and I'll do the damned testing for you. Now get on with it.' The Blue Charms were quite forgotten. I tied him six and he departed, grinning like a schoolboy.

I forgot all about the incident until about three weeks later when I suddenly started receiving requests from people for 'Collyer's Blue', whatever that might have been. I was still puzzling over this when the Skipper showed up, along with a fistful of photographs showing him gloating over some very good fish indeed, all taken on 'Collyer's Blue'. The penny dropped, and I began to fill those orders.

This fly has proved (doubtless by some fluke) to be consistently effective on almost all of the bigger salmon rivers in the UK and abroad. If you catch a salmon on one, do not thank me, just offer up a prayer to the Skipper.

Method of tying

This is a fairly simple pattern to dress, compared with some salmon flies, so for anybody starting out on tying these patterns, it is not at all a bad one to start with, especially as it might winkle out a twenty-pounder.

Fix the hook in the vice and run the tying silk down the shank until you reach almost to the bend, where you catch in a length cf oval gold tinsel and wind a tag of four or five turns. Tie in and trim off the surplus. In front of the tinsel tag tie in another one of gold floss silk and wind it to about the same length as the tinsel one. Build up the tying silk on the shank until it is perfectly level with the tags and then tie in a tail of two golden pheasant crests with an Indian crow substitute feather over the top. The butt consists of three equal parts, black, white and black ostrich herl. After the butt is wound tie in a piece of oval silver tinsel for a rib. Run the tying silk back up the shank almost to the eye and catch in a strand of scarlet floss silk which is then wound down

Collyer's Blue

the shank to the butt and taken back up over the first layer to where it was tied in. Fix and trim. Tie in by the butt a bright blue hackle that has been stripped of its fibres on one side, and wind this down the body. Lock it into position by the turns of ribbing tinsel going up the shank in the opposite direction.

Reverse the fly in the vice and tie in a beard hackle of blue gallena. Turn it right way up again and put on an underwing of two strips of white-tipped turkey tail feather making them fairly wide; on a size 1 hook they should be nearly a quarter of an inch wide. Over this 'stiffener' you place a sheath of married strands of dyed goose (see dressing below) and florican bustard. The married wing is in turn sheathed by folded bronze mallard feather. Along the sides of the fly tie in a pair of jungle cock eye feathers, which should reach about halfway along the wing. On top of these tie in a pair of blue kingfisher rump feathers, and over the whole lot you put two more golden pheasant crests; these should mesh in exactly with the tail so as to form a golden 'halo'. Make a good short head and varnish with sufficient coats to make it smooth and gleaming.

The Dressing (see Plate 8)

Silk:	Black
Tag:	Gold tinsel and gold floss
Tail:	Two golden pheasant crests with Indian crow over
Butt:	In three sections, from the rear: black, white and black ostrich herl
Rib:	Fine oval silver tinsel
Body:	Scarlet floss silk
Hackle:	Bright blue cock
Throat:	Blue gallena
Wing:	Two strips of black, white-tipped turkey tail with a sheath over of blue, scarlet and yellow goose topped by florican bustard. Bronze mallard over this.
Sides:	Jungle cock 'eye' feathers
Cheeks:	Kingfisher rump
Topping:	Two golden pheasant crests
Head:	Black
Hooks:	3/0 – 8, salmon irons